God Wants You to Grow!

God Wants You to Grow!

HOW TO LIVE BEYOND YOUR LIMITATIONS

William D. Watley

Judson Press
Valley Forge

GOD WANTS YOU TO GROW!
How to Live Beyond Your Limitations

Library of Congress Cataloging-in-Publication Data
Watley, William D.
God wants you to grow! : how to live beyond your limitations / William D. Watley.
p. cm.
ISBN 0-8170-1446-2 (pbk. : alk. paper)
1. Christian life. I. Title.

BV4501.3.W375 2003
248.4—dc21

2003040118

Printed in the U.S.A.
10 09 08 07 06 05 04 03
10 9 8 7 6 5 4 3 2 1

To the faithful members, loyal supporters, prayer warriors, extended family and friends that God has given me in St. James

Contents

Acknowledgments

I AM GRATEFUL to my secretary, Mrs. Charlene Diaz, for typing this manuscript. I am thankful to my companion, Mrs. Muriel Watley, as well as Mrs. Gloria Burton, for proofing this manuscript. My adopted sister, Mrs. Carolyn Scavella, who has assisted me in my other books, gave input, as well as did my able assistant, Rev. Raquel St. Clair.

I am indeed blessed for the privilege of serving as pastor to the people of St. James A.M.E. Church in Newark, New Jersey. They have patiently listened to me and faithfully followed me for eighteen years and have encouraged me and prayed for me through the various reincarnations of vision that God has given me and that I have shared with them. We have grown together as we have sought God's vision for our individual lives as well as our corporate life as the people of God.

Introduction

MOVIES, BOOKS, SERMONS, and works of art all tend to revolve around a plot or a central integrating theme or message. The book is no exception to that principle. The central integrating message of this book is this—God has a vision for each of our lives that is greater than any vision that either we or others could possibly have for ourselves. Our responsibility, calling, and mission is to grow to the vision that God has for each of us so that our lives can glorify God in ways that we never envisioned.

Admittedly the genesis for this theme grew partly out of my frustrations as a pastor as I have endeavored to market visions to various individuals and congregations that I have served over the years. There have been times when I have grown impatient because various members of congregations just didn't get what I was trying to say as I challenged them to enlarge their vision of the kingdom of God through the ministry and witness of the local church. Then at some point as I wondered what I was doing wrong, I began to look at the vision that various persons had for their own lives. I discovered that many of God's people have a very small vision or no vision at all for their own lives. Like a bolt of lightning, the thought hit me that if people have a small vision for themselves—their own lives and careers and families—then they would not be able to comprehend a large vision for the church and for the kingdom of God. I discovered that I had been doing ministry in the wrong way for a number of years. I had been trying to get people to have a large vision for the church without understanding the absolute necessity of their first thinking imaginatively, creatively, and largely about their own lives.

I began to see my task as twofold. First, I had the challenge of getting people to think of the graciousness of a God who actually envisioned great things for their lives—things beyond their ability to think, ask for, or even imagine—so that God would be glorified in surprisingly refreshing and profound ways. Then I had the responsibility to connect that vision with the larger vision for the church. It is possible for an individual to have a large vision for self without connecting that vision with the growth of the church and the growth of the kingdom in a local context. God not only envisions for the church, but God also envisions great things for those who are individual members of the body of Christ. God not only envisions great things for the individual member of the body of Christ, but God also expects those members to participate in the life and growth of the church as that congregation lives out the meaning of the kingdom in its local context. The growth of individual members is central to church growth, and conversely the growth of the church is germane to the expansion of vision for individual members.

The messages in this book address an ongoing dialogue and implications of individual as well as church growth. As churches and congregants, we grow individually and collectively as well as spiritually, numerically, and financially for God's glory.

God Wants Us to Grow

TEXT: 2 PETER 3:18

I RECENTLY READ the book *Work in Progress* by Michael Eisner, the CEO of the Walt Disney Company. This book tells the story of Eisner's career, from his entry into the entertainment industry at a low-level, low-paying job to his rise to the leadership of one of the most powerful and respected companies in the world. This book also tells the story of how he expanded the Disney Company from a struggling theme park into a multimedia giant and trend-setter in movies, television, radio, theater, and even cyberspace. His book could easily have been called *Work Completed* or even *Work Perfected* or *A Job Well Done.* He has earned the right to adopt the role of respected elder statesman who could rest upon his laurels and wait contentedly for the day of his retirement.

But such is not the case. In the concluding paragraphs of his book, Eisner states, "As I look around in meetings now, I'm no longer the youngest person in the room. Instead, I've become the one who's looked at for wisdom, maturity, and vision. I do my best to fill the role, but deep down, I don't think of myself that way at all. I feel like a kid, just the way I always have, and I'm relieved that I do." Eisner concludes his book with the statement, "I spend far less time looking back in regret than I do looking forward with anticipation. There is so much to be done."

With all of his success and accomplishments, Michael Eisner still considers himself to be a work in progress. He is an individual who still has a vision for growth. I believe that "work in progress" ought to be the theme or motto of every believing Christian. If there is one thing missing from too many of our lives and from our faith walk, it is a real vision for growth.

After being at this church for over fourteen years, there is still one small sentence I use that strikes consternation in the hearts of even my strongest supporters. That simple sentence is not, "It's tithing time." It's not, "Let me pray over it." It's not even, "Do you love your pastor?" The sentence that drives even my best friends up a wall is this: "I have another vision." Whenever I make that statement people have reactions from, "Oh no, not another one!" to "My Lord, where is he going to try to take us now?" Now I recognize that most of the comments about my visions are made in jest and fun, I think, because a number of people tend to faithfully follow me even though they may not know where I am going. And I appreciate that faith since sometimes I don't exactly know myself!

However, the questions I want to put before some of us today are these: Have you had any visions for growth lately? Have you had any visions for your life, your career, your relationships, your family, your health, or your body lately? And if not, why not? Are you allowing a few disappointments, heartbreaks, and failures to dry up your visioning stream? Are you content with what you have already accomplished? Do you feel you have gone about as far as you can go? Is the theme of your life "Work Completed" or "Work Done" instead of "Work in Progress"?

Who told you that just because you retired from your job that you could not have any more visions for growth? Who told you that just because you have reached a certain age that you are not supposed to have any more visions for growth? Who told you that just because you are divorced or because you are having trouble making relationships work that you could not have any more visions for growth?

Who told you that just because you became pregnant or became addicted or because you spent time in prison or because you have made some mistakes that you are not supposed to have any more visions for growth? Who told you that just because your health or your bodies are not what you desire that you are not supposed to have any more visions for growth? Who told you that just because you have failed a couple of times or fumbled a couple of opportunities that you are not supposed to have any visions for growth? Who told you that because you are physically disabled or because you have had surgery or because you are mentally slower than others that you are not supposed to have any visions for growth? Who told you that because you don't have someone else's looks or experience or background or family connections or money or education or advantages that you are not supposed to have any visions for growth?

When God answers our prayers and helps us to accomplish something, why aren't we saying, "God, I am grateful for what you have done. Now, Lord, I have another vision for growth." When we wake up in the morning instead of complaining about the fact that we have to get up or about our aching back or how tired we are, why aren't we saying, "God, I'm grateful that you brought me through yesterday, but this is a new day, one I have never seen before and one I will never see again. And so for this new day, I have another vision for growth." Why aren't we saying, "God, that last one didn't work out, but I survived, so God, I have another vision for growth." Why aren't we saying, "God, you are still in the blessing business. You still hear and answer prayer. You still make ways out of no ways; you still work miracles. I'm still your child; you still hold me in the hollow of your hands. You still love me; you still will the best for me, so God, here I am again. I have another vision for growth."

A vision for growth is the reason behind our having a variety of choirs who sing a variety of music. A vision for growth started our feeding and clothing ministry. A vision for growth started the scholarship fund. A vision for growth is the reason we keep experimenting with the order of worship. A vision for growth is the reason a part of the worship service is called "the invitation to Christian discipleship."

A vision for growth ought to be what brings us to church. We ought to be coming to church not simply because we have been taught to come or because it is part of our weekly routine. We ought to be coming not simply because we like the preacher or the people or the music or the worship experience. We ought to be coming not simply because we feel comfortable here or because we receive status or have power and recognition here. We ought to be coming here because we want to grow, because we are not satisfied with the way we are, because we realize that we are a work in progress, and because we understand that God's will for us is to grow. Whoever we are, whatever stage in life we are, no matter what we have accomplished, no matter what we may be going through now, God wants us to grow.

Some of us may be going through a bad time. But no matter how difficult the place of transition or trial we may be in, God wants us not simply to go through it but to grow from it. The victory is not simply in surviving; it is being strengthened. The victory is not simply in making it; it is being made anew. The victory is not simply in taking the test; it is being transformed. The victory is not simply in hanging in there—a dead person can hang in there. The victory comes when we reach a new height and see new horizons. Are we doing any growing? Whoever you are and wherever you are, God wants you to grow.

God wants us to grow because growth is a sign of life. Where there is no growth, there is no life. Everything that is alive continues to grow. The tallest and the oldest tree in the world never stops growing. The human body never stops growing. Old cells in the body are constantly dying and new cells are continually being born.

Somewhere between the second and fifth grade I remember opening a geography book and seeing a picture of the Sphinx and the Great Pyramid at Gaza in Egypt. Like a number of you, I cannot recount the number of times I have seen pictures of the Sphinx and the Great Pyramid of Gaza. You can imagine my delight when in 1994 and again in 1997 I had the opportunity to see the Sphinx with my own eyes and actually go inside the Great Pyramid. As ancient as these structures are, they were no taller or wider than they were when they were built thousands of years ago. Why? Because they are stone and stones do not grow because they are not alive. Instead of being works in progress, some of us want to treat life like it is a work of cement or stone. We become comfortable with things as they are, and, like the stone Sphinx and Pyramids of Egypt, we want things to remain the same forever. But if something remains the same, it cannot be alive; it has to be dead, because where there is life there is growth.

That's why some of us have dead relationships, dead religion, dead careers, and dead lives on our hands. We have stopped growing. I fear that when it comes to the matter of our own growth as well as the growth of the church a number of us are being lulled to sleep like the lobster. As we all know, there are two ways to boil a lobster. You can throw a lobster into hot boiling water. But such a way is very painful to the lobster and throws its nervous system into shock. Or we can put a lobster into a pot of cold water and then turn on the fire underneath. In this way the water heats up gradually and the lobster does not realize how hot the water is becoming. Before he realizes it he is boiled and death has come.

That's what has happened to a number of our lives. That's what has happened to a number of our relationships. That's what has happened to a number of churches. That's what has happened to a number of us in our jobs and careers. That's what's wrong with a lot of our religion. We have become so comfortable with where we are that we didn't realize how things where changing all around us. We didn't realize the temperature around us was changing, the culture around us was changing, the attitudes and values and perspectives of those around us were changing. We became comfortable with being the way we were, and we stopped growing. While we were glorifying the good old days and taking pride in what we had done and wanting to keep things at the temperature we have grown accustomed to, the water temperature gradually went from cold to warm to hot to boiling. And now we look up to find that death has come to our relationships, to our careers, to our faith, to our church.

But the good news I bring is that no matter what state we are in, because we are yet alive we can grow from where we are. Before we can grow, however, we first have to know what growth is and what it is not. First, growth is life that comes from within and flows out. We do not grow from the outside in, but from the inside out. Growth is not a matter of improving the wrapping, but rather improving the product. Many of us think we have grown when we do something to the exterior. We come to church more regularly. We may even attend an occasional Bible Study or mid-week service. We are more demonstrative in worship. We clap our hands more. We may even condescend to sing some of that loud praise music or one of those old, dry hymns. We dress differently. We even carry a Bible or at least have one on the desk out in the open. We have learned how to punctuate our speech with an occasional, "Praise the Lord!" We may even give more money in church. It's obvious we have changed. But what have we changed? The product or just the package?

When challenged, are we still inclined to say what we can't do? Do we still panic whenever a crisis arises? Are we still inclined to be negative and expect the worst? Do we still get our feelings hurt at the drop of a hat? Are we still inclined to quit or leave when things don't go our way or when somebody says something negative about us? Do we still fly off of the handle and lose it when something or somebody rubs us the wrong way? Are we still jealous of others who seem to be getting more glory than we are? Does our own insecurity about our looks or weight or education or age still cause us to dislike people who have what we want? Do the people we work with or live with or interact with after the worship is over see any difference in the way we treat them? Are we still falling into the same traps and into the same sins over and over again? Are we still walking by our own wisdom and understanding rather than seeking God's will? Do we still talk about our money as opposed to God's money? The packaging looks good, but have we improved the product? How much growth has taken place from within? Have we spent so much time on the cosmetics of religion that we have neglected to grow the character of religion? As one preacher said, "I'm not talking about your hair; I'm talking about your heart."

The direction of growth must not only be from the inside out, but it must also be forward. Someone has correctly observed that:

> between the airplane and every other form of locomotion and transportation there is one great contrast. The horse and wagon, the automobile, the bicycle, the locomotive, the speedboat, and the great battleship—all can come to a standstill without danger, and they can all reverse their engines, or their power, and go back. But there is no reverse in the engine of an airplane in mid air. It cannot back up. It dare not stand still. If it loses its momentum and forward drive, it crashes. The only safety for the airplane is in its forward and upward motion. The only safe direction for the Christian to take is forward and upward. If he [or she] stops, or if [they] begin to slip and go backward, at that moment [they are] in danger. (From the *Encyclopedia of 7,700 Illustrations* by Paul Lee Tan)

Some of us think that we make progress by looking backward and that we improve by repeating what we used to do. It's all right to look backward to see what has brought us success in the past. But too often we think that all we need to do to improve what is not working is to revive what worked in the past: "We used to do this and we used to do that." But "used to" doesn't satisfy today's needs or pay any of today's bills. When you get ready to make love with somebody you have to do more than talk about what you used to do. We cannot grow by talking about what we used to do. If "used to" was so dynamic, why did it die? Perhaps "used to" died because it had already reached the fullness of its life span. "Used to" can be a good reference point, but it cannot move us forward. It may be a good basement, but it cannot be the main building. "Used to" may be a good anchor, but an anchor is for sitting still, not sailing. When a ship gets ready to set sail the anchor is lifted. They don't throw the anchor away, but neither do they try to sail with it in the water. Trying to grow by holding on to "used to be" is like trying to sail with the anchor in the water. Anchors have their place and purpose, but they are not for sailing.

The truth that we can grow inward from where we are is demonstrated in the words of Peter in today's text: "But grow in the grace and knowledge of our Lord and Savior Jesus Christ. To him be the glory both now and to the day of eternity." When Peter wrote these words, many people of his day were concerned about the Second Coming of the Lord Jesus Christ. Many of the believers expected our Lord to come back during their lifetimes. However, as time elapsed and Jesus did not return, many of the saints became discouraged and began to question when or if the Lord would return. Peter assured them that Jesus would keep his promise, that the day of the Lord would come like a thief. And when that day arrived the heavens would pass away with a loud noise, and the elements would be dissolved with fire, and the earth and everything that is done on it would be disclosed. In the meantime, what was to be the posture of the believer until the Lord returned? Were they to walk around with their heads in the sky looking for Jesus to come back at any moment? Were they to become doomsday prophets declaring to everybody that they needed to repent because the end was near? Were they to consult astrological charts? Were they to consult the Scriptures looking for strange and esoteric Bible codes that would tell them the exact time and place of Christ's second coming?

Peter tells them to wait with patience, to lead lives that become the gospel. He concludes with this word of instruction: *grow.* What do you do when, like Paul and Silas, you find yourself imprisoned in difficult circumstances? Like them, you call on the name of the Lord and hold on to your faith and grow beyond your circumstances. What do you do when, like John on Patmos, you are lonely on your own personal Patmos because the devil has gotten a temporary victory over you? Like John, you look up for a fresh revelation and word from the Lord and grow beyond your Patmos. What do you do when, like Peter, you have made some mistakes and are ashamed to show your face? Like Peter, you receive the good news that we serve a Christ who offers second chances, and you grow beyond your shame. What do you do when, like the women who witnessed the resurrection, people will not believe what you have seen or heard or felt? Like them, you grow beyond the skepticism and doubt, because God will back up what he showed you and fulfill what he has promised. What do you do when, like Jesus, people crucify you when you have done your best? Like Jesus, you understand that Calvary is good growing ground. Calvary is the place from which God will elevate you. Calvary is the place where the devil will once again be proved a liar. And the cross that was supposed to destroy you will become the means of salvation.

With the advent of cyberspace and the emergence of a computer culture, we will grow in our use of technology. With the continued growth of industrial conglomerates, many of us will grow financially. With new temptations to attract us, a number of us will grow in the wrong way. But the basic bent and direction of our growth ought to be to "grow in the grace and knowledge of our Lord and Savior Jesus Christ." And what is grace? It is the unsought and unmerited goodness of God. When you realize that wherever you are and whatever situation you are in the goodness of the Lord is there also, the hand of the Lord is there also, the power of the Lord is present also, then whatever situation you are in is good growing ground to lead you to a deeper knowledge of who Jesus is and who he can be in your life.

If you are sick, that's good growing ground to know Jesus as a healer or as a Savior whose grace is sufficient and whose strength is made perfect in weakness. If you are in sorrow, that's good growing ground to know Jesus as a wonderful comforter. If you are helpless, that's good growing ground to know Jesus as a mighty God. If you are disturbed, that's good growing ground to know Jesus as Prince of Peace. If you are bound, that's good growing ground to know Jesus as the Liberator who sets captives free. If you are in financial need, that's good growing ground to know Jesus as a way-maker. If you are without a job, that's good growing ground to know Jesus as a door opener. If you are lonely, that's good growing ground to know Jesus as a friend who sticks closer than any brother or sister. Grow until the theme of your life becomes "To him be the glory both now and to the day of eternity. Amen."

Do Not Lose Sight of How Big You Can Become

TEXT: JOHN 12:31-33

I BELIEVE THAT GOD has a vision for each of our lives that is bigger than any vision we could possibly have for ourselves. To reach this vision, we are to grow for God's glory, not our own. To reach this vision, God desires for us to grow spiritually, numerically as a church, and financially. Therefore, never lose sight on how big you can become or how much you can grow. A healthy church never loses sight of how big it can become as a body of believers, as a community of faith, as the covenant people of God, as the redeemed. No matter what mistakes or setbacks it encounters along the way, no matter the delays or hardships, negative spirits, or visionless people, it never loses sight of how big it can become for God's glory.

We were not saved for small things. Jesus did not shed his blood on Calvary for us to live mediocre lives that go around in circles, making much ado about nothing. Jesus saved us for big things. Jesus saved us to think great thoughts and to do big things for him, through him, with him, and in his name. The tragedy is that many of us settle for so much less than what God desires for us. Some of us once had a glimpse of how big we could become or how far we could go in life, but somewhere along the way we lost the vision. We became bogged down with mundane problems or we became weighed down with mediocre people, and we lost the vision we once had of big things and far places. Or there were so many obstacles and distractions that we gave up on the vision as fantasy, rather than believing that the vision was something that could actually happen to us.

Perhaps we gave up because the vision seemed too great, beyond our reach. Or maybe it was so long in coming that we grew weary in reaching for it. Or we allowed the temptations of the adversary and the weakness of the flesh to get in the way of the discipline and focus we needed to pursue the big things the Lord showed us. The Lord's message for you today is to stay with your vision. Stay focused on the big things God has for your life. Never lose sight of how big you can become.

Jesus never lost sight of how big he could become. This truth is in evidence particularly in the text when Jesus is talking about the cross: "Now is the judgment of this world; now the ruler of this world will be driven out. And I, when I am lifted up from the earth, will draw all people to myself." Often when we hear this text quoted, we think of lifting up Jesus as an act of worship and praise. How often have we sung or heard it said that we have to lift up Jesus? In the Gospels, those who lifted up Jesus were those who crucified him. They nailed Jesus to the cross and then lifted him up from he earth as he was fastened to the cross. When Jesus mentioned being lifted up from the earth in the text, he was referring to his death on the cross.

That Jesus was talking about his crucifixion when he mentioned being lifted up from the earth is evident from the surrounding verses. The context is not one of celebration but of soberness. Jesus begins it by saying in verse 27, "Now my soul is troubled. And what should I say—'Father, save me from this hour'? No, it is for this reason that I have come to this hour. Father, glorify your name." The passage continues, "Then a voice came from heaven, 'I have glorified it, and I will glorify it again.' The crowd standing there heard it and said that it was thunder. Others said, 'An angel has spoken to him.' Jesus answered, 'This voice has come for your sake, not for mine. Now is the judgment of this world; now the ruler of this world will be driven out. And I, when I am lifted up from the earth, will draw all people to myself.'" Verse 33, the next verse, goes on to say, "He said this to indicate the kind of death he was to die."

What is striking to me about this passage is not Jesus' prophecy concerning his death by crucifixion. Rather, it is the fact that even when he was talking about death by crucifixion, Jesus never lost sight of how big he could become. Even when he was talking about dying on the cross, he saw himself drawing all people to himself. In fact, he saw the cross as something that would help to make him instead of something that would break him. He saw the cross as that which would help him to accomplish God's vision for his life instead of that which defeated God's vision for his life. He saw the cross as that which would glorify him instead of that which would disgrace him. He saw the cross as that which would extend his career instead of that which would end his career. He saw the cross as that which would help him to grow instead of that which would reduce or eliminate him.

This was truly an amazing perspective when we remember what the cross was. As many know, death by crucifixion was a means of capital punishment designed to disgrace and to torture in addition to ending life. It was worse than lethal injections, gas chambers, hanging, or the electric chair, all of which are relatively quick deaths that recognize that even a condemned person has some rights of privacy. In contrast, when a person was crucified, that person was stripped naked and exposed to the public. Because of our sense of modesty and respect, today whenever we see pictures of the crucifixion, Jesus' private parts are always covered with some kind of loincloth. But in reality people were often not covered at all. It is likely that Jesus was crucified naked, with all of his privacy exposed to his friends, his disciples, and his family, as well as to a jeering and hostile crowd. Mary his mother, Mary Magdalene, and the other women standing there, the disciples, and whatever followers were in the crowd saw everything. Crucifixion was meant to inflict both shame on the victim and embarrassment on all who knew him.

Crucifixion was also a very slow and painful death. Sometimes it took days for a person to die by being stretched out and lifted up on the cross, naked and exposed as he baked in the hot

Palestinian sun. That's why in the Scriptures Pilate was so surprised to learn that Jesus was dead in only three hours. Typically, death was so slow and painful that those persons who were being crucified sometimes went out of their minds as they hung on the cross. As the victims of crucifixion were dying, vultures flew overhead because after death the bodies of those circled were left to rot on the cross or thrown onto the ground to become food for wild dogs and other scavengers. We can understand why the followers of Jesus were there to take his body down from the cross and to bury it as soon as he died. They knew what happened to the dead bodies of those who were crucified.

Jesus knew all that death by crucifixion would entail. He knew the pain, suffering, disgrace, and shame that went with death on the cross. Yet he could still look at the cross and keep his vision of how big he could become. To keep our vision of how big we can become requires at least three things. First, Jesus had to be willing to go against the majority opinion or consensus of his surroundings. He had to be willing to walk alone. Secondly, he had to be willing to make some sacrifices. Thirdly, he had to have unswerving faith in the integrity and power of God.

Sometimes to keep the vision of how big we can become we have to be willing to walk alone. Note that I said that Jesus could look at the cross and keep his vision of how big he could become. I did not say that Jesus *and his followers* could look at the cross and see how big he could still become, for those who surrounded him did not share Jesus' perception of the cross. To begin with, those who surrounded Jesus did not share his vision of his ministry or his life. The followers of Jesus for the most part were still following a traditional understanding of his messiahship. They were still hoping that Jesus would overthrow their Roman oppressors and establish an earthly kingdom. And since they were the Lord's handpicked disciples, they envisioned themselves being in positions of power when Jesus came into his own. Since their understanding of who Jesus was and what he was about was wrong, they could not share the Master's understanding or approach to the cross. Peter gave voice to his objections when the Master started talking about dying on the cross, but he was not the only disciple who had problems with the thought of Jesus dying by crucifixion. Since the disciples had hoped to share in Jesus' success, if he failed and ended up getting himself crucified, their futures and careers would also be impacted. After all, some of them had left everything to follow Jesus. When a candidate loses, those closest to him lose also.

Sometimes we will be blessed to have persons around us who also see the vision God has given for our lives. Even if others cannot see it, sometimes they will still support us in it or pray for us as we work toward it. Whatever we have accomplished together in the years I have been the pastor of this church has been accomplished because there were those who either saw the vision of growth themselves or were willing to support the vision they were told about even when they did not see it. However, many times the majority of those in our surroundings will not see what we see. Sometimes the majority of the members of our family or our household, the majority of our friends or colleagues or coworkers or neighbors or fellow church members or worshippers will not see what we see. Thus, many times we will have to go against the majority consensus in our surroundings to hold on to the vision of being big. Sometimes holding on to a vision of bigness will mean that we will have to walk by ourselves.

Never lose sight of your vision of bigness no matter your surroundings or what those in your surroundings might say. You know what God showed you. You know the pictures God has painted and the images God has imprinted in your mind. You know the hunger, the thirst, and the restlessness you have for something bigger and something better. You know the thought that keeps nagging you that there has to be more for you than what you have, than what you presently see and where you are. You know what Scriptures spoke to you when you read them or heard them. You know the promises of God that you are standing upon. So no matter what your surroundings say, never lose sight of how big you can become.

Jesus had to make some sacrifices. To keep sight of the vision of bigness, he had to sacrifice the understanding and support of some of his closest friends, family members, and supporters. To keep sight of the vision of bigness, he had to sacrifice short-term comfort for long-term gains. To keep sight of the vision of bigness, he had to sacrifice his life on a hill called Calvary. In today's world of instant this and instant that, we've got to have it right now. The idea of sacrifice is not very popular. In a world that makes instant millionaires from the lottery and from the Internet, sacrifice is not very popular. In a world of mass marketing that can give a person instant fame and glory, sacrifice is not very popular. In a world of charge it now and pay for it later in easy installments, sacrifice is not very popular. In a world of casual sex and broken vows, sacrifice is not very popular. In a world where the right contacts are considered to be more important than the right education or the right morals or the right work, sacrifice is not very popular.

But the last time I read the Bible the word "sacrifice"—like the word "discipline," like the word "truth," like the word "honest," like the word "obedience," like the word "tithe," like the word "give"—was still in there. That tells me that sacrifice is still part of the Christian life. To get some things in life we are still going to have to make some sacrifices. What is a sacrifice? It is something that costs us something. It is something we give up, even though it means something to us. It is something we cannot part with easily or lightly. It is something we think twice about before we give it up. It entails denying ourselves of something because of our love and desire for something else. If it's something we can easily give up without much thought, then it's not a true sacrifice. If we can give it up and walk away from it without a second thought, it's not a sacrifice. If it's something we do not have to struggle with, pray and agonize over before we part with it, it's not a sacrifice. If it is something we won't miss, it's not a sacrifice. If after giving it up we don't feel it in our heads, our hearts, or our pocket books, it's not a sacrifice.

To keep his vision of bigness, Jesus had to make a sacrifice. Before him stood the devil, who offered him the kingdoms of the world with all of their glory and splendor. Ahead of him stood the cross with all of its suffering and pain. Before him stood the crowd yelling glad hosannas and desiring him to be their king. Ahead of him stood the cross with its loneliness and shame. Before him stood his friends and supporters with their desires for his ministry as well as their personal hopes of good fortune. Ahead of him stood the cross with its distress and pain for all of those who loved him.

Jesus looked beyond the temptations and the comfort and support that were in front of him. He looked beyond death on the cross and saw the vision of a name higher than any other name that God would bestow upon him if he proved faithful, that at his name every knee would bow and every tongue would confess him as Savior and as Lord. So Jesus chose the cross. To the distress of the devil, to the dismay of the crowds, to the disappointment of friends and family, he chose death on the cross. He sacrificed present pleasures for a future promise. He sacrificed short-term rewards for long-term righteousness and gain.

Jesus had to make sacrifices, and we will too. Michaelangelo sacrificed his eyesight as paint dripped in his eyes while he lay on his back to present for the ages the glorious mural of the Sistine Chapel. John Wesley sacrificed his love for books, music, art, and architecture to spend most of his life on saddleback carrying the gospel and planting Methodism everywhere he could. Martin Luther King Jr. sacrificed cushy endowed teaching positions at the leading educational institutions in the land. He sacrificed deanships at prestigious seminaries and universities. He sacrificed comfortable pulpits in big steeple churches. He sacrificed time with his family and long life as a man to die as this country's most dynamic social prophet. And yet years after each of their deaths, their works, their lives, and their names are still held in reverence. It may not be popular to say, but the truth is you don't get much of anywhere in life—and even if you get there, you don't stay very long or enjoy it very much—without some sacrifice. Jesus still says to us, "Whoever does not take up the cross and follow me is not worthy of me. Those who find their life will lose it, and those who lose their life for my sake will find it" (Matthew 10:38-39).

To keep his vision of bigness, Jesus had to be willing to walk alone. He had to be willing to make some sacrifices. And thirdly, he had to have unswerving faith in the integrity and power of God. When you are out there seemingly by yourself, when nobody seems to understand, and those who do understand are not able to help you, you have to know beyond the shadow of a doubt that God is with you, that God will see you through. When you have made sacrifices and hard choices, you have to know beyond the shadow of a doubt that God is faithful and that God rewards those who make sacrifices to pursue God's vision of bigness for them. When you are having a "Calvary moment" and you are stretched out naked and exposed before friends and family and supporters who do not understand, you have to know that God will not disappoint you, that God will bring you through. When you are vulnerable before enemies who are delighting in your struggles, mocking you in your efforts, and hoping for your failure, you have to know beyond a shadow of a doubt in whom you have believed, and you have to be persuaded that he is able to keep everything that you have committed unto him.

When the sun drops its fiery head in the locks of its shoulders at high noon and refuses to shine—and the earth underneath begins to reel and rock like a drunken man—you have to know beyond a shadow of a doubt that God is still in charge, no matter how bleak or hopeless the situation looks. When death comes creeping in the room and stretches its icy hands upon your career, your reputation, your dreams, your heart, your relationships, your household, your church, and even your faith, you have to know beyond a shadow of a doubt that you are God's child. As such you are in God's hands. No weapon formed against you shall prosper, and every wagging tongue that rises in judgment against you God shall refute. When all seems lost and you are buried never to rise again, you have to know that God has the last word, that God is still a God of the resurrection and is still able to restore and give victory to those whom evil has tried to destroy.

Jesus was able to keep his vision of bigness because he had unswerving faith in his Father, who had never failed him. His

Father had been with him in six trials, and he knew that he would not forsake him in the seventh. He knew that his Father willed what was best for him. He knew that his Father would not put more upon him than he could bear. Jesus knew that his Father was faithful and that he had never broken a promise. Jesus knew that his ancestor David had testified, "I have been young, and now am old, yet I have not seen the righteous forsaken or their children begging bread."

A line in the movie *Field of Dreams* refers to going "the distance." If we are to keep God's vision of bigness in view, we have to be prepared to go the distance with God no matter how things may appear at any given moment. Sometimes up and sometimes down, but go the distance. Sometimes leveled down to the ground, but go the distance. Sometimes sick and sometimes well, but go the distance. Sometimes happy and sometimes depressed, sometimes clearheaded and sometimes confused, but go the distance. Sometimes on the mountain and sometimes in the valley, but go the distance. For if you go the distance, God not only goes with you, God will go before you. God will lead you as a pillar of cloud by day, and God will protect you as a pillar of fire by night. To keep the vision of bigness in view, trust God no matter what. No matter what the grapevine says, trust God. No matter what the economist says, trust God. No matter what the statistics say, trust God. Keep your hand in God's hand, and God will bring you out more than a conqueror.

God Wants You to Grow in New Ways

TEXT: ACTS 18:24-28

APOLLOS WAS ONE of the most effective preachers in the life of the early church. He is mentioned four times in the New Testament. There is a brief reference to him in Titus 3:13. He plays a more prominent role in the famous passages of 1 Corinthians 1: 12 and 3:4-6 in which Paul is pleading for unity in the life of that congregation of believers. The Corinthian church had been divided regarding their loyalty to certain pastors or leaders whose teaching and preaching had been instrumental in their development. Apollos, along with Peter and Paul, was one of those mentioned. Today's passage lets us know a little more about this powerful preacher. First, we learn that Apollos was a Jew from Alexandria, located in Egypt. Thus, Apollos was a Jew from Mother Africa. In today's passage Apollos is described as "an eloquent man, well-versed in the scriptures. He had been instructed in the Way of the Lord; and he spoke with burning enthusiasm and taught accurately the things concerning Jesus, though he knew only the baptism of John."

We do not know who introduced Apollos to the Way of the Lord. We just know Apollos received the fruit of someone's work of evangelism. Whoever they were they gave the early church one of its most powerful preachers. However, even though we do not know their names, God knows who they were. Some of us will be in the birthing business. We will birth new believers.

Some of us know of persons who are active in church today because of our influence upon them. We brought them to church. We witnessed to them, we prayed for them, and we ministered to them in a time of need. We encouraged them to accept Jesus as their Lord and Savior. They have become our spiritual offspring. Some of us, in ways we may not even realize, have been instrumental in birthing other persons in the faith.

Let me say here that if there is someone who has birthed you or who has been a major blessing and influence in your life, don't be hesitant in telling them so. Sometimes every believer gets discouraged and wonders if their living is in vain. Your letting someone know that they have been a major blessing to your life may be just the word of encouragement that person needs to hear in that moment of their life. I remember this encouragement during one period in my own career when I was going through turmoil and feeling like a failure. There was an individual who had been an alcoholic who joined church under my ministry and had become one of the strong leaders in his local church. He walked up to me and said, "I am in the church today because of you." That man's comment at that time meant more to me than he would ever know. Whenever I would get discouraged and whenever the devil would tell me that my ministry was not worth very much, I would think of that individual and say, "Well at least that is one thing that I did right. At least there is one life for whom my ministry made a difference."

Some of us will birth new believers, and some of us will birth new ideas and new ministries. Some of us will birth great visions and programs, and, like the person who birthed Apollos as a believer, our names may never get recorded in official church records. No one may ever give us a plaque or a banquet or any other form of human recognition, but our encouragement is that God knows about our contributions. We can say like Job that our witness is in heaven and our records stand on high (Job 16:19). We know that our names are listed in the Lamb's Book of Life and that henceforth there is laid up a crown of righteousness for us that we shall receive when the Lord Jesus shall return in glory, bringing rewards for those who have been faithful.

Whoever taught Apollos the faith did a good job, because Apollos was full of zeal and knowledge. It takes both to be effective. We have to be excited about the Lord, and then we have to be able to explain why we are excited. There are those who have light but no heat. And there are those who have heat but no light. There are those who have the love of Jesus in their hearts, but are mixed up in their heads in what they believe. They have caught the Holy Spirit, but they have not been accurately taught about what they have caught. They can jump up and down with joy, but afterwards they walk a crooked path, not because they are wicked or because they are necessarily hypocritical, but because they have not been taught the correct path to walk. They err because they don't know any better.

Then there are those who know the way and walk accurately in the way, but are as dry as cotton and as dull as watching paint dry. There is very little inspirational about them, very little about them that would inspire someone to follow in their footsteps. They know what they believe, but listening to them is an exercise in patience. Either they put you to sleep in three minutes, or your mind begins to wander within thirty seconds after they open their mouths and you immediately start thinking about how you can escape. There are some people who can take the joy out of anything, including sex. I once had a high school biology teacher who taught our class about the reproductive system and put everybody to sleep. Now you have to be pretty bad to talk to a group of high school teenagers with ripe-and-ready hormones about reproduction and put them to sleep.

Apollos, on the other hand, was both fired up with enthusiasm and filled up with information. His heart was full of the joy of the Lord and his head was filled with information about the Lord. He lived with zeal and taught with accuracy. However, the word tells us that as articulate, as effective, and as knowledgeable as Apollos was, his understanding of the faith was not complete. His knowledge was not in error; it was simply incomplete. He did not believe the wrong thing; his knowledge of the faith simply had some holes and gaps in it.

According to the Word of God, Apollos knew only about the

baptism of John the Baptist. The baptism of John was focused on repentance. Baptism in Jesus' name was focused on rebirth. The baptism of John was focused on rejecting an old way of life. Baptism in Jesus' name introduced a person to a new way of life. It brought that person into the fellowship and life of the church. The baptism of John was focused on running *from* something. Baptism in Jesus' name was about running *to* something. The baptism of John began with condemnation and led to confession. The baptism in Jesus' name began with confession and led to a new creation. The baptism of John focused on death of the old. Baptism in Jesus' name focused on birth of the new. The baptism of John focused on what we used to be. The baptism of Jesus focused on what we could become. The baptism of John was the foundation for baptism in Jesus' name, for repentance must precede rebirth, and confession must precede the new creation. Thus the baptism of John was step one, but baptism in Jesus' name was stage two in the development of a believer. To be a complete believer, we must not only know what we are against, we also have to know what we are for.

Too much of our religion is known by what we are against. A Christian does not do this and does not do that. A preacher is not supposed to do this or the other. That is all well and good, but what does a Christian *do*? What do we stand for and believe in? These days people not only want to know what we are against; they want to know what we stand for. Any idiot can be against something. Even the devil is against something. The devil is against right. The devil is against truth. The devil is against growth. The devil is against God. What are we Christians *for*? It is not enough just to be against abortion. We have to be for life in all of its fullest ramifications. Being for life means that our concern extends beyond the womb to encompass education for those who are born, housing for those who are born, economic well being for those who are born, and quality of life for those who are born. We must not only be against drugs and alcohol; we have to be for freedom. Being for freedom means that we create healthy attitudes that do not cause people to search for false highs when they seek relief. We must not only be against cigarettes; we have to be for health. Being for health means that we honor the body as the temple of the Lord. We are not simply against overeating and bad diets; we are for good nutrition. Good nutrition helps us manage the body, which belongs to God. We are not our own, for we were bought with a price. We are not only against sex outside the bonds of marriage; we are for the standards set by the word of God governing our relationships. We are not simply against gambling; we are for financial health. Financial health puts God first. The key to financial health is honoring God with our tithes and offerings, and with the first fruits of our increase.

Too many of us spend too much energy on what we are against and not enough on what we are for. We can come up with reasons to be against an idea. But we have no idea to offer in place of what we are against. We can tell you why something will not work or will not succeed. But we ourselves have no creative or new ideas or programs to offer unless it is something we did twenty years ago in another era.

Apollos had good training, but it was not complete in that it knew only the baptism of John. As such, he could take people only so far. We can take others only as far as we have gone ourselves. We cannot teach what we do not know, and we cannot lead others where we have not gone ourselves. When we do not grow, we not only affect ourselves, we affect our children, our families, our associates, our friends, and any others whose lives we touch. That is another reason we should want to keep growing. Not only do we desire to go as far as we can, but we don't want to stand in the way of anybody else's growth because we were not able to give them all that is available to them from God.

When Aquila and Priscilla, the husband and wife ministerial team, discovered that Apollos knew only about the baptism of John, they took him aside and taught him the Way of God more accurately. They did not condemn or attack him. They did not dismiss the work he had done or the lives he had touched. They did not find fault with those who had taught Apollos. They simply corrected the gaps in his perspective so that he could grow in his understanding of the Way of the Lord and thereby bring others along with him to a greater understanding and knowledge of the faith. Apollos was a powerful and effective preacher; he just had a few gaps in his understanding of the faith. Everybody has some gaps in their lives. Everybody has some gaps in their faith. Everybody has some gaps in his or her understanding of the Way of the Lord. No matter what our background, no matter how much formal education we have, no matter how long we have been members of the church, all of us have some gaps in our faith.

The Word of God does not tell us about any resistance from Apollos to the teachings of Aquila and Priscilla. Evidently, he was open and receptive to their instruction. Apollos understood that the new things he was learning would help him to grow even more as a believer and to strengthen his effectiveness as a preacher. We would do well to follow the example of Apollos. So many times we get defensive and insulted when new things are brought to us from the Word of God. We think we are insulting our mothers and fathers if we do things differently or see things differently from how they saw them. We think we are insulting the ministers and saints of our childhood or early years as a believer if we add to what they told us or if we change some of the beliefs they instilled in us. We get defensive about our Methodist background or our Baptist background or our Holiness background and feel we are supposed to defend them. If suggestions are made regarding our way of worshipping or singing, we become defensive and start feeling that we are being attacked.

When new teaching comes that more accurately reflects the Way of the Lord or the Word of God, we would do well to receive it like Apollos and to understand that new teaching does not come to criticize what we already have; it is just filling in the gaps. New teaching does not come to tear down our foundation, but to build upon it. New teaching and new ways of worship come to lead us to a new level of growth and maturity so that we can more effectively live as empowered believers. We do not insult those who have gone before us if we add something to what they taught us to fill in the gaps. Tithing, rather than tipping or giving based upon how we may be feeling at the moment, reflects the Way of the Lord. As compared to dinners, bus rides, and other fundraisers, tithing reflects more accurately the Way of the Lord regarding how the church should be supported. Spirit-led giving reflects more accurately the Way of the Lord than reaching into our pockets and grabbing the first thing we lay our hands on or getting rid of our loose change.

Praise and worship that follows the leading of the Spirit rather than the bulletin or printed program reflects more accurately the Way of the Lord than simply going through the motions or our routine. Change more accurately reflects the Way of the Lord than simply doing the same things the same way with the same people all the time. Growth more accurately reflects the Way of the Lord than staying in the same old rut for the rest of our lives.

Apollos was a fine preacher and an effective evangelist before he met Aquila and Priscilla, but when they taught him about the baptism of Jesus, he grew in new ways. God wants us to grow in new ways. We grow when we expand our minds with new teachings, new visions, and new ideas. We grow when we expand our faith with new challenges and new problems. One of the great attributes of God is that God can take the things that the devil sends into our lives to break us and instead grow us in new ways. Therefore, every time the enemy sends something into our lives to break us, instead of asking God why, instead of feeling sorry for ourselves, perhaps our prayer ought to be, "Lord, use this problem to grow me in new ways for your glory."

Nobody likes to get sick. Sickness is not the will of God for God's people. Sickness is either the result of our own mismanagement of our bodies or the attack of the adversary upon these bodies, which are temples of the Holy Spirit. So when sickness comes, as we pray for healing, let us also remember to pray, "Lord, use this disease to grow my spirit, my soul, my strength, and my reliance upon you in new ways." When the enemy invades our homes and attacks our relationships, our children, and our companions, as we pray for victory, let us also remember to pray, "Lord, use this attack to grow me in new ways for your glory. In this attack grow my patience. In this attack grow my faith. In this attack grow my dependency and my trust in you." When our careers are in turmoil and our jobs are in trouble, as we pray for deliverance, let us also remember to pray, "Lord, use this trouble to grow my testimony to your glory."

When relationships fall apart and marriages end in divorce and we pray for power to go on, let us also remember to pray, "Lord, use this divorce to grow my determination in new ways to your glory." When death takes a loved one, as we pray for strength to bear up under the load and face all of our tomorrows, let us also remember to pray, "Lord, use this sorrow to grow my strength in new ways to your glory." When sin causes us to fall short of the glory of God, as we pray for forgiveness, let us also pray, "Lord, use this sin and stumbling to grow your salvation in new ways to your glory." When we become bound and addicted to what has gotten out of control, as we pray for our freedom, let us also remember to pray, "Lord, use this mistake and this mess to grow a new miracle in my life to your glory."

After Aquila and Priscilla taught Apollos the things concerning Jesus, he was even more effective in his preaching and in his teaching. He was a new and improved Apollos. When we receive new instructions in the Way of the Lord, and when we allow God to grow us in new ways, we become new and improved. Every now and then we will go to the store and pick up a product that we have used before, and we will see on the package the words "New and Improved." The words are letting us know that something has been added to the product so that, as good as it was, as reliable as it was, now it will work even better, taste even better, clean even better. The product may look the same, but it is not the same; something has been added on the inside that makes it "new and improved."

That is what growth is all about. That is what receiving new instructions in the Way of the Lord and the things concerning Jesus, the Holy Spirit, tithing, the Scriptures, worship and praise, and the Word of God is about. That is what allowing God to grow us in new ways is all about. We may look the same, but we are not because something has been added to our minds and our faith, to our souls and our spirits, that makes us new and improved. We can love even better and forgive even more because the new instructions and God's Word and will have been added to our lives, making us new and improved. We can have more joy and generosity in our living, our giving, and our service. We can be more effective in our praying and in our witnessing. We can go back to work with a different walk; we can go back to school with a different talk; we can go back home with a different attitude; we can deal with relationships with a different strength; we can even come to church with a different spirit, because new instructions and God's Word and will have been added to our lives that have made us new and improved. There are any number of degrees that we can attach to our names, but there is one degree that every child of God can have. And that is the N.A.I. degree—New And Improved.

During his lifetime, Jesus was very effective as a preacher and teacher, and also as a dispenser of power. He had the power to speak and the howling wind would cease to blow. Rolling billows would lie down and be still. He had such power that the masses could be fed with two fish and five barley loaves. He had such power that he could speak and lepers would be cleansed, the lame would walk, demons would cry out and flee, the blind would see, and the dead would be raised to life.

The devil determined that he would break the Lord's power on a hill called Calvary. But God decided he would use Calvary as a way of strengthening Jesus' hand. Thus, when God raised Jesus early Sunday he raised him New and Improved. Jesus arose to declare, "All power in heaven and in earth is in my hands. I can destroy, and I will defend" ("Go Preach My Gospel," hymn based on Matthew 28:18). Jesus arose New and Improved as King of Kings and Lord of Lords who reigns forever.

And today he says to all of us that we can all be better. We can all be New and Improved. We can think differently. We can live differently. We can give differently. We can love differently. We can be free. We can be victors instead of victims. We can be stronger. We can be happy and joyous.

Do Not Let Anything Stop Your Growth

TEXT: MARK 16:1-7 AND LUKE 24:28-35

"I CAN'T BELIEVE I did such a thing. How could I do such a thing? He said I was going to do it, but I didn't believe him. I just could not have imagined I would ever do such a thing. I am so embarrassed and ashamed. I have made such a fool of myself. How can I ever show my face in public again? How can I ever go around the disciples again? What will my friends and companions think of me now? Will they ever accept me back into their fellowship or forgive me? More importantly, will Jesus my Master and best friend ever forgive me?"

These were probably some of the thoughts that entered Peter's mind immediately after he denied knowing the Lord on the night Jesus was betrayed and turned over to his enemies. To refresh our memory, when our Lord was betrayed by Judas and turned over to his enemies in the Garden of Gethsemane, the other disciples forsook him and fled. According to Matthew's and John's accounts, Peter had made an effort to defend the Master by cutting off the ear of Malchus, the servant of the high priest. And as our Lord was led away by the mob that had come to arrest him, Peter followed him, but at a distance.

While our Lord was being questioned and tried in the residence of the high priest, Peter was standing outside in the crowd warming himself by the fire when someone accused him of being a follower of Christ. Peter promptly denied knowing Jesus. Later on someone else identified Peter as a disciple of Jesus, and again he promptly denied knowing Jesus. Yet a third time Peter was identified as a follower of Jesus, and for the third time he denied knowing Jesus. According to some accounts, Peter cursed and swore that he did not know Jesus. According to Luke's Gospel, at the very moment of his third denial, Jesus turned and looked directly at Peter. Then Peter remembered our Lord's prediction that before the cock crowed that very day Peter would three times deny knowing the Lord. Then Peter immediately went off by himself and wept bitterly.

I would imagine that the night of his denial of Jesus was the worst and loneliest night that Peter ever spent in his life. He had before made a number of blunders and had embarrassed himself on any number of occasions. Even a casual reading of the Gospels reveals Peter's inclination to have foot-in-mouth disease. However, all of his efforts, faults, and failures notwithstanding, his denial of Jesus was by far his most grievous, embarrassing, and shameful act.

During the course of our lives we all make a number of mistakes, any one of which could wreak havoc with our lives and our faith. But there are some that stand out as the most embarrassing and shameful that, more than all the others, have the potential to wreck our faith, our lives, our careers, our families, our marriages, and our relationships. Some wounds cut more deeply than others. Some exposures cause more embarrassment than others do. Some things, if they were to come to the light of day, would cause more shame than others would. Some things seem almost unforgivable and unrecoverable in the sight of others if they were ever discovered.

How do you continue to hold your head up and continue to function as a husband, wife, friend, father, mother, relative, minister, teacher, doctor, lawyer, social worker, professional, or president when your hand has been caught in the "cookie jar" and everybody knows it? How do you continue to look people in the eye when your business is out in the street and everybody knows it? How do you relate to people knowing that they know some of your private failures but not knowing what they are thinking when they are looking at you in the eye? When the truth gets out and you cannot deny it any longer, how do you look at people in the face when you know and they know that you have betrayed their trust in you? What do you do when you feel lower than low? That was the reality Peter faced on the night in which he denied knowing the Lord.

Perhaps that was why Peter received his own personal invitation to behold his risen Lord in Mark's account of the message that the angels delivered to the women who went to the tomb to anoint the body of the Lord on that first Sunday after the Lord's crucifixion. According to the text, the angels told the women to "go, tell his disciples and Peter that [Jesus] is going ahead of you to Galilee; there you will see him, just as he told you." Peter's pain and shame were so deep—and God was so loving and forgiving—that the angels called his name specifically to let him know that he was forgiven and that Jesus still loved him. And if anyone asked him how he could dare face Jesus after what he did, Peter could always say that he was there because he was personally invited to behold his risen Lord. The words of the text were also an invitation for Peter to grow beyond his shame and his pride and to maintain his place of leadership in the fellowship where he belonged.

What is significant to me is not just that Peter was personally invited to stay in the fellowship of the disciples, but that Peter accepted. An invitation, after all, is no good unless it is accepted. We know that the invitation was good and that Peter did not allow his shame to keep him away from the disciples, because that very evening of the first resurrection in Luke's Gospel we are told that two of the disciples were walking from Jerusalem to the village of Emmaus, which was a few miles outside of the city. Jesus started walking with them, but they did not recognize their Lord, and as he joined their conversation, beginning with Moses and the prophets, he began to teach them the things about himself found in all the Scriptures. As they approached the village, Jesus walked on ahead as if he was going on, but they urged him to stay with them for the evening. When they were at the table, Jesus broke bread, blessed it, and gave it to them.

When they saw him breaking bread at the table, their eyes were opened and they recognized him. They reflected for a moment how their hearts had been burning as Jesus talked with them on the road and opened the Scriptures unto them. Then in that same hour they returned to Jerusalem, and when they found their fellow disciples gathered together they gave them the news: "The Lord has risen indeed, and he has appeared to Simon!" Evidently Simon Peter had moved beyond his shame, because when the Lord appeared to him he was in fellowship with the other believers.

Whoever you are and whatever your name is, you have a personal invitation from Jesus to grow beyond where you are. Whatever your background, whatever your past, no matter what mistakes you have made, hearts you have broken, hurt you have caused, or persons you have disappointed, you have a personal invitation from Jesus to grow beyond where you are. However you are dressed, whatever your present circumstances, whatever your gender or race, you have a personal invitation from Jesus to grow beyond where you are. However well you may be doing right now, you can be doing better. Whatever accomplishments you have already achieved, I tell you that you can still accomplish more with Jesus than you can accomplish on your own.

You, like Peter, have a personal invitation from Jesus to grow beyond where you are. Whoever you are, the Lord has sent me here with a message just for you that says, "Tell the church assembled and Peter and Mary and John and Richard and William and Joan and Susie and Helen and Robert and Rasheed and Theresa that I have risen from the dead and that I have gone ahead in glory to prepare a place for them. But if they reach out to me as their Savior and follow my word, they will know me as their friend and Lord. When they call I will answer. When they stumble I will catch them. When they fall I will pick them up. When they get dirty I will clean them. When their way is blocked I will make a way for them. When they cry I will comfort them. When they have needs I will bless them. Tell the church assembled—Jennifer and Donald and Charles and Carole and Latifah and James and Marian—that they matter to me, that I love them and that I want them to grow beyond what they see for themselves. I want them to grow in new ways to God's glory."

My heartfelt counsel to you today, whoever you are and whatever your name, is not to let anything stop your growth. Peter did not let his shame stop him from growing. Don't let your shame stand in the way of your growth. I suspect there are many persons who are letting shame keep them away from the church and from the Lord's gracious invitation to grow. So you made a mistake. Who doesn't? So you made a fool out of yourself. Who doesn't? So you let some people down, disappointed some people, hurt some people along the way. Who doesn't? So you disgraced yourself at some point. Who doesn't? Everybody has a closet that says on the door, "Please, please do not open," because of what's hidden inside. Don't let your shame stand in the way of your growth.

Closely related to shame is pride and ego. Some of us are overly concerned about what other people will think or say if we show up or come to the Lord. We don't want to have to confront certain people. We are too stubborn to admit that we are wrong, and we are too proud to apologize. I shudder to think of the relationships that have ended because of pride, because both persons refused to budge on some minute point, or because both persons refused to be the first to pick up the phone and make a call even though both parties were in misery. How many of us will not go back to school and how many of us are in danger of losing jobs because we are too proud to admit what we don't know and thus will not get the training that is available? How many of us are constantly making fools of ourselves, showing our ignorance and giving out misinformation because we are too proud to admit that we don't know? How many of us are missing out on the help we need because we are too proud to go to the people who can help us because we don't like them or they are younger than we are or have less formal education than we have? How many of us are drowning in trouble and addictions because we are too proud to admit that we need help?

How many of us are quenching the Spirit of the Lord because we are too proud and too concerned about what others might think or say if we openly praise the Lord? We forget that the people we are trying to impress have no hell to put us in and no heaven to take us to. We forget that many of the people we are trying to impress are far from perfect themselves and that many of them are worse off than we are. Many of their relationships are in trouble; their homes are out of control; their children are unruly; they cannot keep their own mate satisfied or settled; they are living above their means; their bills are about to drown them; their careers are on the skids and they are hanging on to their jobs by a thread. They are unhappy and frustrated themselves; they can hardly get a prayer through themselves. So why are we trying so hard to impress them? Why do we need their judgment to validate us? Do not let pride and concern about the opinions and judgments of others stand in the way of your growth!

Do not let shame, do not let pride, and do not let logic stand in the way of your growth. It was not logical that Peter should be given another chance after denying Christ three times in a row, but he was. It was not logical that he should be given a personal invitation to see the risen Christ, but he was. It was not logical that Christ should not wait to meet him in Galilee but that he should appear to him as he walked on the road to Emmaus, but he did. Quit trying to figure everything out. Faith, God, the Bible, the gospel are not always logical, but they are still true. Don't try to figure everything out. Just believe whatever you can of the Good News and grow from there. Taste and see that the Lord is good. Not all truth is logical. It is not logical that the great God of the universe should be concerned about us, as small and insignificant as we are in the grand scheme of things. But it is true nevertheless. It is not logical that God should love us so much that God should come in human flesh, whose name is Jesus, and be subjected to one of the most inhumane and painful deaths that human beings have been able to devise—death on a cross—in order to save us from sin. But it's true. It is not logical that we should be given second or third and even fourth and fifth chances after what some of us have done and continue to do, but it is true. It is not logical that at the point where some of us are in life that we can be born again and become new creatures, but it is true. It is not logical that after enduring all he did on earth that Jesus will come back to the same earth that once crucified him, but it is true. Jesus is coming back again for those who have been faithful.

And it is not logical that tithing works. Bring the full tithes and offerings into the storehouse. It may not be logical, but it works. Give and it shall be given unto you—may not be logical, but it works. The wings of the bumblebee are not logical, but they work. When one considers the size of the body of the bee and the size of its wings, it is thermodynamically impossible for the bee to fly. Yet bees fly every day. It is not logical that black and brown seeds can produce a fruit that is green on the outside, that is separated by a white rind from a red inside. Yet watermelons grow every day. It is not logical that something as ugly as a caterpillar can become something as beautiful as a butterfly. Yet they do. It is not logical that two chemicals as flammable as hydrogen and oxygen can be combined to produce water, which puts out fire. Yet they do. It is not logical that two poisonous substances like sodium and chloride can be combined to make salt, but it does. Tithing may not be logical when you have bills to pay, but it works. It works because God said it would.

We will not be able to grow to our fullest when we rob God. Those who hold back on God do not receive all that God has to offer to them. Those who hold back on their tithes and offerings, those who hold back on giving in obedience to the Word of God, those who hold back on praise, those who hold back on surrendering all and on being totally available to the Word and will of God and the work of the Holy Spirit within and upon their lives, those who hold back on their obedience and their commitment, do not receive all the growth God has for them.

Peter did not let his failure to live as he should stop him from responding to heaven's gracious invitation to grow beyond his weak moment. Are we allowing our favorite sin or habit that we are still clinging to stop us from receiving all of the growth that God has in store for us? What I said about tithing also holds for some of the things that some of us continue to do. We will not receive the full growth that God has for our lives until we turn our back on some sinful relationships and involvements, until we let go of the habits that abuse and enslave our bodies and hold our minds and our spirits in captivity. Whatever it may be, it is not worth sacrificing the vision—the salvation and the growth God has for your life. Whoever they are, they are not worth sacrificing the vision—the salvation and the growth God has for your life.

Do not let anything and do not let anyone stop your growth. Some of us have talents and gifts that we should be giving to the Lord. Some of us have service that we should be giving to the Lord. Some of us know that we should be more involved in the church than we are, but we are letting our feelings about certain people stop us from growing in the service of the Lord. We don't like the preacher. We don't want to work with this one or that one. Somebody hurt our feelings. We don't think people like us. We don't want people to talk about us. Well let me ask you a few quick questions: Who woke you up this morning? Who gives you health and strength every day? Who answered your prayer when you called out in trouble, and who blessed you with what you stood in need of? Who keeps you day by day as you journey through mean streets? Who brings you back safely to your home? Who healed you when you were sick? Who made a way for you when your path was blocked? Who helps you pay your bills when your money runs short? Who is with you when you are lonely, and who steps in with just what you need just when you need it the most? Why, then, are you allowing someone else to stop you from serving God who has been so good to you and denying yourself the growth that comes from serving God?

Do not let anything or anyone stop your growth. Peter didn't, and don't you do it either. Go, "tell his disciples and Peter that [Jesus] is going ahead of you to Galilee; there you will see him, just as he told you." That very evening when Jesus showed up on Emmaus Road, Peter was where he was supposed to be, in fellowship with the disciples. He did not waste any time accepting heaven's invitation to grow beyond his shame, his pride, his failures, and his worries about what others thought. Don't you waste any time either. The time to move beyond your shame is now. The time to start letting go of your pride is now. The time to start giving as you should is now.

The time to turn your back on some things is now. The time to start receiving the fullness of what God has in store for you is now. The time to be born anew is now. The time to start giving your all to Jesus is now. The time to repent and to begin living anew is now. The time to take your eyes off of other people and start putting them on Jesus, who loves you and who died to save you, is now. The time to believe the promises of God for your life is now. The time to accept God's vision for your life is now. The time to yield to the moving of the Holy Spirit is now. The time to join the church is now. The time to renew your vows and commitment to the Lord is now. The time to start wailing in boldness is now. The time to start living victoriously is now. The time to leave guilt and fear behind is now. The time for growth is now. Do not let anything stop you.

Are You Ready for Growth?

TEXT: LUKE 5:1-11

EVERY DAY SOMEONE fishing in the seas of life comes up with an abundant catch. And every day someone else fishing in those same waters comes up with nothing. Every day someone makes a fortune, and every day someone else loses one. Every day someone experiences a breakthrough, and every day someone else experiences a breakdown. Every day, one person's yoke is broken while another enters into bondage. Every day someone experiences growth and transformation and change for the better, and every day someone else continues in a monotonous, routine, dull, joyless, frustrating, uncomfortable, no-growth pattern lifestyle.

I happen to believe that God desires the best and wills the best for God's children. There is an old song that says, "Stars belong to everyone, the best things in life are free." I don't know about the best things in life being free, but this I believe—that God wills the best things in life to the people of God. Unconditional love, peace of mind, joy of spirit, salvation of the soul, health of body, wealth of pocketbook, power to persevere, victory over sin, abundance of opportunities, defeat of the devil, conquering of obstacles, unexpected blessings from above, goodness and mercy that follow us for the rest of our lives, soundness of relationships, solid family life, quality and longevity of life here and eternal life hereafter—those are the best things in life. Whether we receive them or not depends on whether we are prepared to grow to receive all that God desires for us.

Most of us have probably heard people pray, "Lord, you have been better to us than we have been to ourselves." Not only has God been better to us than we have been to ourselves, but God probably desires more for us than we want for ourselves. You have heard me say before that one of the great frustrations of being a pastor is seeing more for people than they are prepared to see for themselves and wanting more for people than they want for themselves. Bishop T. D. Jakes once wrote a book in which he asked the question, "Can you stand to be blessed?" The issue I want to raise is whether we are prepared to receive all that God is prepared to bring into our lives.

In the text, Jesus is beside the Lake of Gennesaret and is looking for a suitable place to teach the crowds that are pressing in upon him. He saw two empty fishing boats at the shore whose owners were nearby washing their nets. He got into the one belonging to Simon Peter and asked him to pull out a little ways from the shore. Then, using the boat as his classroom and pulpit, our Lord taught those who had gathered to receive what he had to offer. Allowing the Master to teach from his boat was such a little thing for Simon Peter to do. Simon Peter had no idea of the tremendous life-transforming experience he would have by simply allowing the Master to use his boat for a little while. We never know the long-range import of our little actions. Words such as "yes" and "no" are little words. But depending upon how they are said, when they are said, and to whom they are said, they can affect our lives as well as the lives of others. That's why we have to be so careful about what we do and what we say. If there is one thing that we as God's people are not careful enough about, it is what we say to whom. New members and young people and even seasoned saints who may be passing through a difficult season of their lives do not need to hear some of the negative things some of us are prone to say and repeat. The little lie that we tell, the little, catty innuendoes, the gossip and rumors we pass around, the little criticisms we make of others may be all someone needs to hear to cause them to leave the church.

Conversely, a little word of encouragement can keep someone on the right road. And years later they will call you blessed because your little word of encouragement or your little act of kindness was just what they needed at a very critical moment. A smile is a small action, but it can often accomplish more than a major speech. Saying "thank you" or "I'm sorry" are small actions, but they can go a long way toward winning and keeping the hearts of others. Getting dressed to come to church and walking down the aisle to join others can be such little actions, but they can change the whole course of life. A little more time in prayer on a daily basis is a small action, but it can bring untold blessing to our lives. A little more time in Bible study is a small action, but it opens up whole new worlds.

Simon Peter's allowing Jesus to use his boat was a small action, but look what it yielded in his life. Never forget that great growth comes from small things, small actions, small beginnings. Great lives come from small sperm and eggs. Great oaks are born from small acorns. Today we travel through space because one day somebody looked at a bird and asked a small question: "I wonder if humans can fly." One evening a man who had a pregnant wife asked an innkeeper if he had any room for them. The innkeeper said he had no room, but they could stay in his animal shelter. Such a small action, but it had momentous implications. Whoever would have known that centuries later we would still be singing and talking about the fact that the first cradle of Jesus Christ, the Savior of the world, was a manger, an animal-feeding trough? One day on a little hill outside of the city of Jerusalem a small group of people observed the execution of three men who were being crucified. After the one in the center died, they were hurriedly taken down from their crosses and buried so that the city could go on with its annual major celebration known as Passover. On Sunday morning several women went in the dark to the tomb of the man who had hung on the middle cross and discovered that the tomb was open and the body of Jesus was gone. From that small execution and that small mystery of the open tomb and the missing body grew the most powerful faith statement that humanity has ever heard, which is this: We as humans not only have the victory over the devil and sin, but we also have victory over death and the grave.

One day Jesus walked up to a fisherman who was washing his nets and said, "I need a boat from which I can teach these people who have gathered to hear me. May I borrow yours?" Peter said, "Of course you can." From that small action, Peter's life would never be the same. After Jesus had finished teaching the people, he turned to Peter and said, "Because of your willingness to let me use what you have, I am going to bring some growth into your life. I'm going to bring a blessing into your life that you aren't prepared to receive. Put out into the deep and let down your nets for a catch." In the Old Testament, to receive the growth that God would bring into his life, Abraham had to be prepared to move his tent to unfamiliar territory. To receive the growth that God would bring into his life, Moses had to return as God's spokesperson to Egypt, from which he had fled as a fugitive. To receive the growth that God would bring into his life, David had to leave his father Jesse's household. To receive the growth that God would bring into her life Rebecca had to leave her older brother Laban's household, and Ruth had to leave her native land. To receive the growth that Jesus was preparing to bring into his life, Peter had to be prepared to move into some deeper waters.

How prepared are we to move to deeper waters to receive the growth God desires to bring into our lives? A two-hour worship service a week and that's it in terms of our involvement with church and with the Lord is pretty shallow water. Now shallow water will keep our boats afloat. But to receive the growth God wants to bring into our lives, we have to be prepared to move into deeper waters.

To get to the deeper waters meant that Peter had to spend more time in the presence of Jesus. To receive the growth that God wants to bring into our lives, we have to make more time for the Lord. A grace over meals or a hurriedly said prayer in the morning or at night or when we are on our way to our next appointment is pretty shallow water. Now shallow waters will keep our boat afloat. But to receive all that God desires to give us, we have to journey with the Lord to deeper water. We have to make more time for the Lord.

Reading the Bible only when we come to church, or reading the same passages of Scripture over and over again, or picking up the Bible and trying to find something to read when we are in trouble or when we are trying to find comfort is pretty shallow water. Now shallow water can keep us afloat, which is where most of us are in terms of our religious life. We are afloat, but we are not moving to deeper water. And to receive all that God desires to give us, we have to move into deeper waters. And that means spending more time in the presence of the Lord. When it comes to giving, anything less than ten percent of our gross income is shallow water. Now shallow water can keep us afloat, and that is where many of us are: financially afloat. When we are just making it from paycheck to paycheck and month to month, we're just afloat. When we are always playing catch up and dodging bill collectors, we're just afloat. When any unexpected expense sends us into a panic, we're just afloat. When we're always rushing to the bank trying to cover checks, we're just afloat. To receive all that God desires to bring into our lives, we have to move to deeper waters, and that means spending more time in the presence of Jesus.

Somebody might be saying to himself or herself, "What more does he want? I'm doing the best that I can." First of all, most of you are not. You know it and God knows it. Secondly, the issue is not what I want, but what the Lord requires in order to take you to the next level. To graduate from any kind of school, you have to meet certain requirements. To get or keep any kind of job, you have to meet some kind of requirements. To get a driver's license you have to meet certain requirements. Church work and our service to the Lord are the only areas of life where we feel that whatever we do and whatever we give ought to be good enough. But the Lord is saying to us today that to receive all that God desires to give us, we have to meet certain requirements. We have to be willing to move from the shallow where we are and journey with him to some deeper water.

We can't handle the demons that arise in our lives, because we are not deep enough in the Word of God, we are not deep enough in prayer, we are not deep enough in our worship and praise of God, and we are not deep enough in the things of the Spirit. Some of us say to ourselves, "I'd like to go deeper, but I'm so busy. How do I make time for the Lord?" The same way we make time to sleep, we make time for the Lord. The same way we make time to eat, we make time for the Lord. The same way we make time to talk on the phone or watch TV, we make time for the Lord.

We all could do things other than the things we do. People go to church not because they have nothing else to do, but because they made the time to do it. In the same way, we all need to make more time to be with the Lord. We schedule it in. If we have to get up earlier or stay up later, or if we block out an hour or two during the day, we become intentional about scheduling time with the Lord. God is too important in our lives for us to always be in a hurry when we are talking with him or to always try to catch God on the run.

Steven Covey, in his book *The Seven Habits of Highly Effective People*, cites a famous illustration about time management. It is the illustration of a person who was going to fill an empty jar with rocks. So he put large rocks in first. Then he put in smaller rocks around them. And then even smaller rocks around them. Then he fills the remaining empty places in the jar with sand. When he asks the point of the illustration, most people (including me) respond that the point is that we are to keep the empty places in our lives filled. But that's not the point of the illustration. The point is that we begin to effectively manage our time by putting in the big rocks first. What are the big rocks in your life? I imagine that our jobs are one. I imagine that children and family are one. I imagine that friends and social life are one. But be sure that God is the first big rock and that before we schedule anything else, we devote at least an hour or more to God each day. We have twenty-four hours in the day. A tithe of our time would mean that God deserves 2.4 of those hours. Can't we begin to work on what is due to God by devoting at least one hour of every day to time alone with God through prayer or Bible study, not simply reading but study or meditation. That's how we begin to move into deeper waters.

When Jesus told Peter to move into deeper waters, Peter replied, "Master, we have worked all night long but have caught nothing. Yet if you say so, I will let down the nets." No matter what kind of past we have had, we need to know that God has an abundant future and a glorious harvest and great growth for us. I don't care how many times you have tried and failed, God has an abundant harvest and a glorious future for you. I don't care how many relationships have failed, or how many times you tried to kick the habit and failed, or how much time and energy you have given in the past and failed, God still has an abundant harvest and a glorious future and great growth for you. Perhaps, like Peter, our problem is that we were out there fishing on our own without Jesus being in our boat. We were relying on our own strength and good intentions. We were relying on our own experience and knowledge of the waters. Perhaps, like Peter, we were out there on the water ahead of Jesus. Sometimes we can ask God to help us do certain things, and before God can move or act we run ahead on our own and try to catch fish our way. We try to land a man or a woman our way. We try getting the victory our way. We like to deal with people and get even with people our way. We are trying to run some of these church ministries and church programs our way.

Or perhaps, like Peter, we've been fishing in the wrong place. Young women and young men, be careful where you drop your nets. Mature and middle-aged people, be careful where you drop your nets. You may be lonely and feeling desperate, but be careful about where you drop your nets. Saints who have a generous spirit, don't be gullible. Be careful about where you drop your nets. Don't cast pearls before swine. Don't drop your nets until the Word of God and the Spirit of God tells you. Or perhaps, like Peter, your timing will be off. Whenever we are relying on self or others and not on the Lord, our timing will be off. Jesus always knows the right place and the right time and the right conditions to bring in the harvest, to bring in the growth and the increase.

When Jesus spoke to Peter, he didn't ask him about his failures of the past. How long Peter had fished and where he had fished was not of importance to Jesus. Jesus had a blessing for him. Jesus had growth for him. Jesus had a harvest for Peter right then if he was willing to travel with him to deeper waters. That's the good news that I bring to you again and again. No matter what your past has been or what your present is like, Jesus has some growth for you right now. Jesus has some power for you right now. Jesus has some healing for you right now. Jesus has some salvation and deliverance for you right now. Jesus has a harvest for you right now. Jesus has a new life for you right now. Jesus has some greater blessings for you right now. Jesus has some friendship and some forgiveness for you right now. Jesus has some love and some companionship for you right now. Jesus has a ministry for you right now.

Peter said to the Lord, "We have worked all night long but have caught nothing. Yet if you say so, I will let down the nets." Growth happens when we are ready to obey the Word of God without reservation. Peter did not ask for a sign; he just obeyed. Peter did not try to bargain or negotiate with Jesus saying, "Perhaps I will just cast one net out and see what happens." He obeyed, and cast his nets out. God knows where the fish are and God knows what we need. Are we prepared to believe and follow the Lord's Word simply because it is the Word of the Lord? The issue is not whether we like the messenger. The issue is whether or not we are prepared to believe and obey the Word of God. The issue is not whether or not we like our fellow believers or the other passengers in the boat. It is whether or not we are prepared to believe and obey the Word of the Lord. The issue is not whether we agree with all of the policies or programs of the boat. It is whether or not we are prepared to believe and follow the Word of the Lord. The issue is not who hurt our feelings or mistreated us or did not cooperate with us or who doesn't like us. The issue is whether or not we are prepared to believe and obey the Word of Jesus. The issue is not even whether the instructions are logical or whether or not they make sense. The issue is whether or not we are prepared to believe and follow the Word of the Lord. Growth does not happen and the harvest will not come until we are prepared to take God at God's Word.

I don't know how far out in the waters they traveled or what they talked about as they traveled, but evidently when they reached a certain point Jesus turned to Peter and said, "Drop your nets right here." Remember, the Lord knows where the fish are. You may have gone past some spots that looked like choice spots to you and wondered why the Lord didn't tell you to cast your nets there. But remember the Lord knows where the fish are. There may not be any fish in the spot that looks so good and promising from the surface. The chosen spot may look barren to you, but the Lord knows where the fish are. You may have already fished there and caught nothing, but if the Lord tells you to drop your net in that same spot, do it because the Lord knows where the fish are. The spot may not be your first choice of places to fish, but the Lord knows where the fish are. And if the Lord tells you to drop your net right there, just obey. The spot may appear unpromising to you, but if the Lord tells you to drop your nets there, just do it.

According to the text, when Peter and his associates lowered their nets in obedience to the instructions of Jesus, they received such a multitude of fish that their nets began to break. They signaled to their partners in the other boat to help them. But the haul of fish was so great, not only did their nets begin to break, but their boats began to sink. Are we really prepared to receive all that God is prepared to put into our nets and pour into our boats? Are our nets of faith strong enough to hold all of the growth God is prepared to pour into them when we take God at God's Word? Are our boats of obedience prepared to hold all of what God will put into them when we follow where we are led? Are our nets of perseverance strong enough to hold all that God will pour into them when we hold out until breakthroughs come? Are our boats of prayer strong enough to hold all that God will pour into them when we live a life of prayer? Are our nets of humility strong enough to hold all that God will put into them without turning our heads and hearts away from the Blesser? Are our boats of forgiveness large enough to hold all of the blessings God will pour into our lives if we can grow beyond some things that have happened to us in the past?

Remember that God is always ready to bless beyond our capacity to receive. God is always able to bless more than we are able to receive. God is always prepared to grow us more than we want to grow. God is always ready to take us farther than we want to go. God is always ready to stretch us farther than we want to be stretched. The question we have to answer is, "How much do we want to grow?" God will grow you as tall and stretch you as far as you are prepared to grow.

When Peter saw the multitude of fish, he fell to his knees and said, "Go away from me, Lord, for I am a sinful man!" But Jesus responded to him and said, "Do not be afraid; from now on you will be catching people." He says the same thing to us when we are hesitant about being stretched and about growing beyond our comfort zones: "Don't be afraid. Trust me. I love you, and I want the best for you. I'm not going to hurt you; I'm going to help you. I'm not going to burden you; I'm going to bless you. I'm not going to break you; I'm going to build you. I'm not going to trouble you; I'm going to take care of you. I'm not here to mess you up; I'm here to make you. I'm not here to add to your problems; I am here to multiply your pleasures. I'm not here to cause you suffering; I have come to give you salvation. I'm not here to cause you loss; I am here to give you life."

When Peter reached the shore, he left everything and followed Jesus right then. Are we prepared to follow Jesus right now? The journey to growth and wholeness begins right now. Not next week or next month or next year, but right now. Not when we get back to our regular church home, but right now. Not when we have some things in our lives to straighten out, but right now. Not when we are dressed differently, but right now. The journey to transformation and power begins right now. The journey from bondage to deliverance and from earth to heaven can begin right now if we are prepared to follow Jesus all the way. Are you ready to grow?

Preparing for Growth

TEXT: ACTS 1:4-5

EVEN A CITY BOY like me knows that when you get ready to plant anything, you don't just drop a handful of seeds on the ground and expect much of anything significant to grow. Even a city boy like me knows that before one plants anything, one has to first prepare the soil to receive the seed. First, the soil has to be turned over, and if there are any stones or broken glass or trash in the ground—which is a very real possibility when you are turning over soil in a city lot—then the waste has to be taken out and discarded. Then the soil is fertilized with compost or other organic substances. Then a trench is dug, or as they used to say in the country, you "lay the row" to receive the seed. Then you plant the seed. Even a city boy like me knows that no matter how good the seed is, the soil must first be prepared if one expects to see growth.

For three years Jesus had been dispensing seeds to his disciples. In Luke 9:1 we are told that Jesus "called the twelve together and gave them power and authority over all demons and to cure diseases, and he sent them out to proclaim the kingdom of God and to heal." These were seeds of power and authority over demons and disease. They were seeds of the gospel, which is the proclamation that God reigns. Evil does not reign, nor violence, nor fear, nor guilt, nor our weaknesses, nor our addictions, nor other human beings, nor corporate conglomerates, nor nations, but God reigns.

The seeds given to the disciples had the potential for birthing a new age and growing a new world and a new humanity for God. He had given them the command to grow such a world. Luke 24:47 tells us that Jesus had commanded the disciples to proclaim repentance and the forgiveness of sins to all nations in his name, beginning in Jerusalem. However, to grow the kind of world and the kind of people Jesus had envisioned, Jesus knew that the seeds he had given to the disciples had to first take root in their own lives.

In Acts 1:4-5 Jesus is preparing the disciples for growth: "While staying with them, he ordered them not to leave Jerusalem, but to wait there for the promise of the Father. 'This,' he said, 'is what you have heard from me; for John baptized with water, but you will be baptized with the Holy Spirit not many days from now.'" Jesus knew that in spite of the disciples' time with him, many of their hearts needed to be turned over or turned inside out. Jesus knew that fear, doubt, misunderstanding, confusion, hurt feelings, personal agendas, and wounded egos needed to be removed and discarded from their spirits. Jesus knew that some trenches needed to be dug—rows or furrows needed to be laid—in their thinking and in their vision and perceptions so that there would be receptivity for seeds of growth, improvement, transformation, and development. Thus, Jesus told them that before they went anywhere and tried to develop anybody, they were to stay in Jerusalem to receive the fertilization they needed, which was the baptism of the Holy Spirit. Before they could grow to the vision Jesus had for them, they had to be prepared for growth.

Let me just remind all of us again that God has a vision for each of us that is greater than anything that we could ever envision for ourselves. Think of the greatest thing you could ever imagine happening to you, and know that God has a vision for your life that is greater than that. Our visions are bound by time, but God's vision for us stretches into eternity. Our visions often center on that which is material or that which we can hold in our hands. God's vision for us is not only about physical needs and some of our wants. It includes that which can hold us when material things wear out, run down, and have no meaning. Our vision includes prosperity in some things. God's vision for us includes blessings and prosperity in all things.

Our visions are often short-sighted, and they often put what ought to be first in last place and what ought to be last in first place. God's vision for our lives puts everything in its proper place and sequence. Our visions are often about glorifying self, but God's vision for our lives points to a God who is greater than any of us could ever conceive. Our vision for ourselves is dependent upon what neither we nor other humans can do. God's vision for us means that we have as our resource the very power that lit the sun and hung the stars. Our visions are bound by our limited power, but God's vision for us means that our power is linked with God's unlimited power. Our visions are defined by what we can see or conceive, but God's vision for us goes beyond what we think or imagine.

But before we can receive all that God envisions for us, we have to be prepared to receive it. The questions I want us to focus on are: Are we prepared as a church and are we prepared as individuals to receive all that God has for us? How do we prepare for growth, for God's vision for our lives? In the text, Jesus commanded the disciples to stay in Jerusalem until they received the promise of the Father, which was the baptism of the Holy Spirit. And the disciples obeyed. The first step in our preparation for growth is obedience. We cannot receive the fullness of God's vision for our lives by talking about doing our own thing or how we did it our way. That's why our lives, our bodies, our relationships, and our faith are in the shape they are in now. We did our own thing with them and to them, and we treated them our way. We cannot grow to or receive the fullness of God's vision for us when we are disobedient to the Word of God.

When the Word of God tells us to love God with all our hearts and all our souls and our entire mind, obey. When the Word of God tells us to seek first God's kingdom and its righteousness, with the assurance that all we need will be given to us, obey. When the Word of God tells us to pray without ceasing, obey. When the

Word of God tells us to glorify God with our bodies because we are not our own as we have been brought with a price, obey. When the Word of God tells us to be anxious for nothing, but in everything with thanksgiving to let our requests be made known to God and the peace of God that passes understanding shall keep our hearts in the knowledge of Jesus Christ, obey. When the Word of God tells us to resist the devil, not run to him, and he will flee from us, obey. When the Word of God tells us to bring the full tithe into the storehouse so that there will be meat in God's house, obey. When the Word tells us to put God to the test and see that God will pour down an overflowing blessing, obey. When the Word of God tells us to honor the Lord with our substance and the first fruit of our increase with the promise that our vats will overflow, obey.

Obedience to the Word of God prepares us for growth. And obedience to the Holy Spirit prepares us for growth. Ephesians 4:30 tells us, "Do not grieve the Holy Spirit of God, with which you were marked with a seal for the day of redemption." When the Holy Spirit moves you in worship to do something different, obey. When the Holy Spirit moves you in worship to just relax and let go and let God, obey. When the Holy Spirit is nudging you and convicting you and pulling you and telling you to join church, obey. When the Spirit is telling you to leave where you are and go where you are being fed and fulfilled—no matter how long you have been where you are—obey. When the Spirit is telling you to quit checking the temperature or the current or the depth of the water and to just step in, obey. When the Holy Spirit plants a vision in your spirit and a thought in your mind, obey. When I was a boy we used to sing, "When the Spirit says move, you gotta move." Obey.

Obedience to the Word of God, to the Spirit of God, and to the leadership that God has sent to us prepares us for growth. Hebrews 13:17 tells us, "Obey your leaders and submit to them, for they are keeping watch over your souls and will give an account." In Jeremiah 3:15 God says to his people, "I will give you shepherds after my own heart, who will feed you with knowledge and understanding." When God sends you good pastors—whether young or old, male or female—don't pick them apart. Don't go around trying to find whatever you can that is negative on them so you can spread it abroad. Don't laugh or mock their visions. Don't sit in the seat of the scornful and knock everything they try to do. Don't go around saying, "I don't have to listen to them because they are just a man or a woman like me." Or, "They are not as young or as educated as I am." Maybe so. But God didn't call you to be a shepherd. God called them. Preacher fighters and rebellious spirits do not grow. They do not receive the fullness God has for them. When God sends you good leaders and shepherds, pray for them. Support them. Work with them. Uphold their arms in battle. Follow and submit to them as they follow and submit to God.

The disciples were obedient to the Word and the leadership of Christ because they had faith in their Lord. They stayed in Jerusalem as Jesus told them to do and they trusted Jesus enough to obey his Word simply because he said so. When I was growing up, my parents used to say something that infuriated me, and I promised myself that if I ever grew up and had children that I would never say it to them. Sometimes when my parents would tell me to do something I would ask why. I must admit that often they really would try to explain things to me. But there were times when I had plucked their last nerve, and they would simply say, "Because I said so." It would irk me to no end. But when I had my own children and I would tell them something to do and they would ask me why, there were times when I became my parents all over again, and I would look at them and say, "Because I said so."

Part of our preparation for growth is the same kind of respect for the authority of Christ. But beyond that, we will need faith in the integrity of Christ, the love of God, and the nurturing of the Holy Spirit. We have to know that God loves us, and Jesus cares for us, and the Holy Spirit desires the best for us, so that whatever we are told "to do" we simply do it because they said so. Sometimes the Holy Spirit will move us or plant something in our spirits and we will not understand why. We will not understand why we are led to help certain people or to pray for certain people or why certain people weigh so heavily upon our spirits. We won't understand why we are drawn to certain churches or ministries or certain pastors or certain people. We won't understand why we are led to turn down some offers and accept others after we have prayed about them. We won't understand why certain visions come to us. We won't understand why we are not satisfied with mediocrity or why what is good enough for others is not good enough for us. We won't always understand why we demand excellence.

But faith in the leading of the Holy Spirit and the Word of God means that we reach a point where we say, "Lord, I don't understand why you are leading me to this place or why such a thing is weighing so heavily upon me, but if you say so I am prepared to follow. If you say so I am prepared to give them another chance. If you say so I am willing to try again. If you say so I am willing to put down my roots right here. If you say so I am willing to change my plans for my future and my career and to walk where you lead me. If you say so, even if my loved ones and family do not understand, I will go back to school or make this career move. If you say so I will change, even though I am comfortable where I am or being the way I am. I have fished all night long and have caught nothing. But if you say so, I will let down my nets one more time. I have tried and tried again and again and have accomplished nothing, but if you say so I will keep on trying. I have been knocking on door after door—and door after door has been closed in my face—but if you say so, I will keep on knocking. I have tried time after time to kick this habit, and I have grown weary of hearing myself ask for mercy and pleading for another chance. I am beginning to feel that my situation is hopeless and that I have to live with this weakness. But if you say so I will keep fighting until the victory is mine, until recovery is mine, until the weights and the sin that so easily beset me have no power or hold upon me anymore."

And when others come up to ask us why we are doing or not doing certain things, we have to believe in prayer, in the Holy Spirit, in the Word of God enough to say, "Because the Lord says so." Why are we tithing and giving to the Lord off the top when we don't know how we are going to pay our bills? Because the Lord says so. Why do we keep trying to do the right thing when the wicked are prospering all around us? Because the Lord says so. Why do we keep coming to church when we are not recognized and the pastor does not even know our name? Because the Lord says so. Why do we keep praying for certain people? Because the Lord says so. Sometimes all we can say is, "I don't know *why*, but I know *whom*. I know that Jesus loves me. I know that the Holy Spirit wants what is best for me. I know that God has not brought me this far to leave me. I know that God would not lead me up a blind alley or lead me wrong. I know what the Spirit showed me. I know that Christ will keep his word and fulfill his promise. I have faith in the word of God. I have faith in the love of Christ. I have faith in the leading of the Holy Spirit. So if the Word says so, if the Lord says so, if the Spirit says so, that is all that I need to go on."

We prepare for growth through obedience. We prepare for growth through our faith in the goodness, the Word, and the love of Christ for us. We prepare for growth by being open and available for whatever growth God wills for us, for whatever growth the Lord Jesus sends and the Holy Spirit fosters. Remember that when Jesus told the disciples to stay in Jerusalem until they received the promise of the Father, which was the baptism of the Holy Spirit, they did not know what to expect. Because we have read the story we know about the Day of Pentecost. We know how the Holy Spirit filled the place where they were like the sound of a rushing and mighty wind. We know how cloven tongues of fire appeared over each of their heads. We know how they began to speak in other languages as the Spirit gave them utterance. We know that Peter received such an anointing that when he preached under the unction of the Holy Spirit three thousand souls joined the church. We know about the aftermath of Pentecost; we know of the many signs and wonders performed by the apostles. We know about all they did and all that happened to them after they received the Holy Spirit. But when Jesus told the disciples to stay in Jerusalem, they did not know what to expect. Even so, they were open and available to receive whatever the promise of the Father was. They were open and available to receive whatever the Lord intended for them. They were open and available to receive whatever God was giving out. They were open and available to receive the baptism of the Holy Spirit, whatever it meant.

Being prepared for growth means being open and available for whatever the Lords sends. We never know how God is going to grow us. God may grow some of us into missionaries and others of us into preachers. God may grow some of us into teachers and others of us into business people for his glory. God may grow some of us who don't think that we can pray or speak or sing in public into such boldness that we will be able to do in public what we thought we would never be able to do. God may grow some of us into financial as well as spiritual prosperity. God may grow talents in some of us that we did not even know were there. God may grow some of us into new professions or jobs or locations. God may grow some of us out of certain relationships and into new relationships. God may grow some of us into being single, saved, and satisfied. God may grow some of us into new ways of worship and praise. We cannot say to God, "Grow me in this way but not in that way. Grow me in prayer but not in giving or tithing. Grow me in faith but not in forgiveness or patience. Grow me in the supernatural but not in love and caring." Being prepared for growth means being open and available to however the Lord seeks to grow us and use us. Being prepared for growth means saying, "Any way the Lord blesses, I'll be satisfied."

"While staying with them, [Jesus] ordered them not to leave Jerusalem, but to wait there for the promises of the Father. 'This,' he said, 'is what you have heard from me; for John baptized with water, but you will be baptized with the Holy Spirit not many days from now.'" Being prepared for growth means being obedient. It means having faith in the intentions of Christ for us, and it means being open and available to however the Lord chooses to grow us.

But preparing for growth must begin now. Many are still waiting for any number of reasons to receive the Lord's invitation to grow.

Some of us are still saying, "I plan to join, but before I do there are some things I want get straightened out in my life." Church is not for those who have it all together; church is for those who are still trying to get it together. Church is not for those who have everything straightened out, but for those who are still trying to straighten some things out. Church is not for the perfect but for the imperfect. Church is not just for harvesting fully-grown plants; it is for planting seeds. If you already have your life together and everything straight, then this is not the church for you. We are in church not because we have it together, but because we are trying to get it together. We are recovering liars. We are recovering adulterers and fornicators. We are recovering thieves and gossippers. We are recovering backsliders and hypocrites. We all have some issues and hang-ups and things we are working on and working through. And like anyone who is in the process of overcoming, we make mistakes. We stumble and fall, and we mess up sometimes.

But because we are in church and in Christ, when we stumble we know that we can get back up. And when we make mistakes we know that if we call upon the name of Jesus we will be forgiven and given another chance. Because we are in church and in Christ, we know that even when we are at our most unlovely, God still loves us and God still sees something of value in us. Because we are in church and in Christ, even when we feel most alone we know that we really are not by ourselves, that God in Jesus Christ is with us and the Holy Sprit is closer to us than breathing, nearer than hands and feet. Even with all that we are not, we are growing. Even in our mistakes we are growing. We will be the first to admit that we are not all we should be, that we are not all that we are going to be. But we also have a testimony that says we are not what we used to be. We are growing.

The time for your growth is now. Not next week, but now. Not when you are stronger, but now. Not when you are dressed differently, but now. Not when you have straightened some things out in your life, but now. The rest of your life begins right now. The journey from earth to heaven and from strength to strength begins right now. The path to peace in your spirit and joy that is overwhelming, everlasting, and full of glory begins right now.

Charlotte Elliott (1789–1871) was a vibrant young lady who lived a carefree life, gaining popularity as a portrait artist and writer of humorous verse. By the time she was thirty, however, her health began to fail rapidly, and she soon became bedridden and depressed. But God still had a vision for her life. And so one day a friend came to her and said, "You must come as you are, a sinner, to the Lamb of God that taketh away the sin of the world." Charlotte Elliott received Jesus as her personal Savior and began to grow into a writer of religious hymns from a sickbed that she was confined to for over fifty years. Fourteen years after her conversion she wrote a hymn—"Just as I Am, Without One Plea"—that has been a blessing to many souls that have received the message that they, too, can begin growing into power and into a new creation right now:

Just as I am, without one plea, But that Thy blood was shed for me,
And that Thou bidst me come to Thee, O Lamb of God I
come, I come!

Just as I am, and waiting not To rid my soul of one dark blot,
To Thee whose blood can cleanse each spot, O Lamb of God I
come, I come!

Just as I am, though tossed about With many a conflict, many a
doubt, Fightings and fears within, without, O Lamb of God, I
come, I come!

Just as I am, Thou wilt receive, Wilt welcome, pardon, cleanse, relieve;
Because Thy promise I believe, O Lamb of God, I come, I come!

Amen.

How to Grow

TEXT: 2 PETER 3:18

AT ONE TIME or another every believer comes to God and asks the question, "God, what is your will for my life? Should I go left or right? Shall I move, or shall I stay where I am? Should I marry this person or not? Should I accept the promotion or this new job or not? God, what is your will for my life?" I cannot answer the question of what God's will is in a specific situation, but this much I know: God's general underlying will is that we grow. Whatever situation we are in and whatever decision we make, God wants growth from it or through it. Sometimes we choose wrongly. Everybody at one time or another makes errors in judgment. However, even in the worst decisions we make, if we can grow from them, our time has not been wasted. Some of us can testify that some of our greatest lessons and some of our greatest growth came from mistakes in judgment and wrong decisions. We learned some things about others and ourselves—and about life itself—that we could not have learned any other way. God may not have willed that the path to our learning be as painful as it was, but God does will that some growth come as the result of our pain. God wills growth for us because growth is integral to life, and where there is no growth, there is no life.

But the question I want to consider is, "*How do we grow*?" How do we grow as individuals? How do we grow as a church? After all, not only do all living things grow, but they also grow in particular ways. Vines grow in one way; trees grow another.

Vines grow sprawling all over the ground, and trees grow straight up. And if we ever saw a vine growing straight up or a tree grow by sprawling all over the ground, we would say that something was wrong. We would call such a vine or tree a freak or aberrant or strange. Turnips grow one way, and corn grows another. Turnips grow under the ground, and corn grows on top of the ground. And if we ever saw a stalk of corn growing under the ground and a turnip growing on top of the ground, we would pronounce such growth strange and aberrant.

Butterflies grow one way while bees grow another. Butterflies begin life as ugly, slimy, crawling caterpillars. Only after a period of time in a cocoon does a metamorphosis occur that transforms them into the beautiful winged creatures that glide in the air. And if a butterfly ever skipped the caterpillar stage, we would say that something was strange or wrong or aberrant or freakish about its growth.

All living, believing Christians grow because wherever there is life there is growth. The issue is *how* we are growing. Our text, the word of God, clearly tells us how we are to grow. It says, "But grow in the grace and knowledge of our Lord and Savior Jesus Christ. To him be the glory both now and to the day of eternity. Amen." I submit to you that a number of us are growing, but we are not growing according to this biblical mandate. And thus we are growing in ways that are aberrant, strange, wrong, even freakish. Whenever I see a believer who claims to be pro-life but who supports capital punishment and war, that is freakish. You can't be protective of life in the womb and destructive of life after it comes forth from the womb. Whenever I see pro-life supporters willing to murder persons who perform abortions and willing to destroy clinics where abortions are performed, that's freakish. Whenever I see so-called pro-life supporters vote against education money, affirmative action, and other social programs that enhance the quality of life for those who are living, that's freakish. That's like supporting caterpillars and supporting butterflies, but condemning cocoons. Pro-life ought to mean a commitment to an abundant life from the womb to the tomb to the resurrection.

The conservative Christian right is wrong. Its politics and methods of intimidation are as iron-fisted, bare-knuckled, and vicious as any secular or worldly organization. It thinks nothing about smear, smut, and falsifying the truth and lies to get its point across. It is mean-spirited, without mercy. It is arrogant and without the anointing. It knows the law, but does not know love except for its own. It represents the very kind of exclusionary, self-righteous, prideful, arrogant Pharisee-ism that Jesus condemned with some of the harshest language in the Gospels. It is simplistic, facile, and shallow. It caters to those who want easy answers to complex problems. It preys upon the worst fears of those who believe that we face the future by nostalgia and by recalling the so-called good old days of "Gone With the Wind."

Such growth is aberrant and strange for those who claim to follow Jesus, who was compassionate, who was inclusive, who was a friend of sinners, who forgave a woman who was caught in adultery, who gave a much divorced woman living water, who cast out demons from a hopelessly possessed man, and who granted access to Paradise to a dying thief. Such growth is aberrant and strange for those who claim to follow Jesus, who fed the hungry, who touched the untouchable, who met people where they were so that he could take them to where they should be, and who refused to use the methods of this world to fight his battles. Such growth is strange and aberrant for those who claim to believe in someone who taught and practiced love and forgiveness, patience and tolerance, self-denial and the way of the cross, and prayer for our enemies, and who taught that those who exalt themselves will be humbled and those who humble themselves would be exalted, that the first would be the last, and that the meek—not the mighty—would inherit the earth. Such growth is aberrant and strange for those who claim to follow Jesus, who proclaimed, "The Spirit of the Lord is upon me, because he has anointed me to bring good news to the poor. He has sent me to proclaim release to the captives and recovery of sight to the blind, to let the oppressed go free, to proclaim the year of the Lord's favor" (Luke 4:18-19).

Such is the Jesus of Richard Allen. Such is the Jesus of Harriet

Tubman. Such is the Jesus of Sojourner Truth. Such is the Jesus of Fannie Lou Hamer. Such is the Jesus of Rosa Parks. Such is the Jesus of Martin Luther King Jr. Such is the Jesus of Jesse Jackson. Such is the Jesus of Andrew Young. Such is the Jesus of Nelson Mandela.

We are to grow in the grace and in the knowledge of our Lord and Savior Jesus Christ. How are we growing? Many of us are growing in the knowledge of local church culture, but are we growing in our knowledge of our Lord and Savior Jesus Christ? Every church has its own personality, its own traditions, its own culture, its own politics, and its own style and way of doing things. We have joined the "We don't do that here" club. We may be learning the names of the so-called movers and shakers and what bases we have to touch to get things done. We may even be making a name for ourselves as one of the leaders or potential leaders of the church. We may have picked out our favorite seat, our favorite service, our favorite choir, our favorite project, and our favorite people. Some of us have decided our place in the church: "I'm a background person" or "I'm a leader." "I want the pastor to know my name and who I am" or "I really don't care if he knows me or not as long as I get fed." "I want to be involved in the church" or "I just want a good worship experience on Sunday morning." We have learned the most often sung hymns, praise songs, and anthems. All of this is well and good, but unless it is accompanied by growth in the grace and knowledge of Jesus Christ, it is still growth that is aberrant and wrong.

Some of us are growing in length of membership in the church. We will tell you with pride how long we have been members. That's all well and good, but are we growing in the grace and knowledge of our Lord and Savior Jesus Christ? Some of us are even growing in our knowledge of church gossip. We can tell you what we heard about what certain people are rumored to have done back in the day. Or we can tell you the latest juicy tidbit about who is supposed to be doing what and with whom. Such knowledge will make us popular with a certain crowd. Of course when we have trash to empty, a garbage can is always popular. Or when we have to go to the bathroom, a commode is popular. Or during a flood, a sewer is always popular. Such knowledge will make us popular if that is how we desire to be known and used, but anyone who is growing in that way is growing in an aberrant and freakish way. We can grow in any number of ways even in church, but are we growing in Christ as we grow in our involvement in the life of the church?

I fear that many of us have the same problem Paul's people had when he wrote in Romans 10:1-2, "Brothers and sisters, my heart's desire and prayer to God for them is that they may be saved. I can testify that they have a zeal for God, but it is not enlightened." What God said through his prophet Hosea (4:6) also applies to so many of us: "My people are destroyed for lack of knowledge." Many of us have great zeal for the Lord and for the church, but it takes more than zeal for growth; it also takes knowledge. What is killing our growth and causing so much confusion in our own faith journey as well as in the life of the church is our lack of knowledge. That's why our text tells us to "grow in the grace and the knowledge of our Lord and Savior Jesus Christ."

As believers we need more than an inspired heart; we also need an informed head. We not only need the Spirit; we need study. We not only need salvation; we need substance. We not only need a testimony; we need truth. We not only need edification; we need explanation. We not only need excitement; we need education. We not only need experience; we need enlightenment. We not only need faith; we need facts. We not only need intensity; we need intelligence. We not only need compassion; we need content. We not only need redemption; we need reflection. We not only need religion; we need refinement. We not only need love; we need light. We not only need conversion; we need clarity.

As Christians, our faith is grounded in the grace of God, which is the unsought and unmerited goodness of God. That's what Paul was talking about in Ephesians 2:8 when he said, "For by grace you have been saved through faith, and this is not your own doing; it is the gift of God." In 2 Corinthians 8:9 he reminded the church that "you know the generous act of our Lord Jesus Christ, that though he was rich, yet for your sakes he became poor, so that by his poverty you might become rich." We as Christians have good grounding, and good grounding ought to produce good growth. Strong roots ought to produce a strong plant. Many of us have strong roots. We were raised in the church. We have strong roots. We have been running this race a long time. We have strong roots. We have an active relationship with the Lord Jesus Christ. We have strong roots. We have great testimonies about what we have seen the Lord do personally in our lives. We have strong roots. We even have a solid prayer life. But with all of that, are we growing as we should? Are we coming into our fullest measure and maturity as followers of the Lord Jesus Christ? We can live with somebody and still not know him or her. We can work with and for others and still not know them. We can talk with someone every day and still not know him or her. How well do we know the Lord Jesus Christ? It is our lack of knowledge of the Lord Jesus Christ that prevents the riches of growth from taking place in our lives. Nothing takes the place of knowledge, and where there is no knowledge there is no growth. We can lay out prostrate before the Lord all night long, but nothing takes the place of knowledge, and where there is no knowledge there is no growth.

Saul of Tarsus had good grounding, but because he did not have a proper knowledge of Jesus he started off fighting those he should have been affirming. Peter had good grounding, but because he didn't have the proper knowledge of Jesus he denied the one he should have been supporting. John the Baptist had good grounding, but because he didn't have the proper knowledge of Jesus he second-guessed the One he should have been sure about. Thomas had good grounding, but because he did not have the proper knowledge of Jesus he doubted the One he should have trusted with his whole life. Judas had good grounding, but because he did not have the proper knowledge of Jesus he betrayed the very one to whom he should have remained true.

"But grow in the grace and knowledge of our Lord and Savior Jesus Christ. To him be the glory both now and to the day of eternity." When we come into a proper knowledge of who Jesus is as Lord and Savior, we are not as susceptible to the many false doctrines and strange teachings that cross our paths. The issue of strange and false teaching was also of concern to Peter in this letter. In chapter 2:1-4, he wrote:

> But false prophets also arose among the people, just as there will be false teachers among you, who will secretly bring in destructive opinions. They will even deny the Master who bought them—bringing swift destruction on themselves. Even so, many will follow their licentious ways, and because of these teachers the way of truth will be maligned. And in their greed they will exploit you with deceptive words. Their condemnation, pronounced against them long ago, has not been idle, and their destruction is not asleep.

In 2 Timothy 4:3-4, Paul also addressed the rise of false teaching. He wrote: "For the time is coming when people will not put up with sound doctrine, but having itching ears, they will accumulate for themselves teachers to suit their own desires, and will turn away from listening to the truth and wander away to myths."

Our lack of knowledge about what we should believe about Jesus Christ has produced aberrant, strange, and freakish growth among us. This notion that all religions, all churches, and all preachers teach the same thing is not true. Be clear that not all religions, churches, and preachers are the same. They do not espouse the same doctrine. Not all religions, churches, and teachers teach the Lordship of Jesus Christ, that he is God in human flesh and can save us from our sins, and that to him belong glory now and to the day of eternity. Jesus is more than a great teacher like Buddha; Jesus is Lord and God, and to him belongs glory now and to the day of eternity. Jesus is more than a prophet like Mohammed; Jesus is Lord and God in human flesh, and to him be glory now and to the day of eternity. Jesus is not to be equated with the Dalai Lama; Jesus is Lord and God, and to him belongs glory now and to the day of eternity. Christianity is not the same thing as New Age philosophy or a collection of insights from some mythical Celestine Prophecy.

Christianity is the teaching and praxis of Jesus, who is Lord and God in human flesh but who has now ascended to heaven and to whom belongs glory now and to the day of eternity. Because Jesus is Lord to whom belongs glory now and to the day of eternity, because he alone was found worthy to redeem us from our sins and release us from the eternal bondage of death, we are not bound by Levitical dietary laws and practices as the Jehovah Witnesses would have us believe.

Some churches and preachers do not lift Jesus crucified, raised, reigning, and coming back as the central focus of their teachings. They lift themselves or they emphasize the teachings of some founder or leader as much as they do Jesus. Or they lift some teaching or doctrine or passage of Scripture as the basis of their faith. But as Paul reminds us in 1 Corinthians 3:11, "For no one can lay any foundation other than the one that has been laid; that foundation is Jesus Christ." We are saved and have hope of eternal life not because of the way we were baptized or because we received the gift of tongues or because of the Holy Communion or Eucharist or because of any apostolic succession or historic episcopate or because of congregational polity or local church autonomy.

> [Our] hope is built on nothing less, Than Jesus' blood and righteousness; [We] dare not list the sweetest frame, But wholly lean on Jesus' name. On Christ, the solid Rock, [we] stand; All other ground is sinking sand, All other ground is sinking sand. ("My Hope Is Built," Edward Mote)

You can't swallow hook, line, and sinker everything you hear on the radio or see on the television or read in a book or a magazine. Some of what you hear will produce freakish and aberrant growth. So how do we receive proper knowledge? First, we need to become affiliated with a body of Christ called "church," with a shepherd who is anointed and prepared. Being a Christian is not a Lone Ranger experience. It is about being in fellowship with a body of believers with whom our own spirits blend, who will help direct our growth. And you cannot be a member of a body of believers without being under the leadership and authority and direction of some shepherd. It is the shepherd who leads, feeds, and guides the flock. A flock without a shepherd becomes a wild herd. It is the shepherd who receives the vision for the flock and then leads the flock according to that vision. It makes no difference how long you have been a member of the flock; you are not the shepherd.

Then you need systematic, sustained, and directed Bible study. Individual Bible study, while necessary, does not do it alone. You can be attacked by all kinds of strange spirits and assaulted by all kinds of strange ideas and concepts as you study the Word by yourself. You may need more background knowledge than you have to correctly understand and interpret what you are reading. That's why you need guided Bible study by the church. Reading a passage of Scripture only during worship service produces aberrant growth. One weekly sermon cannot equip you with all the information you need to grapple with the issues of life. To grow in the grace and knowledge of our Lord and Savior Jesus Christ, we have to study the Word of God and see what it says about Jesus. When you study the Word of God under the direction of a Christ-centered church and a prepared and balanced shepherd, you will not be so easily led astray by every strange wind of doctrine.

One of the advertising slogans of a certain clothing manufacturer states, "An educated consumer is our best customer." A believer who studies the Word of God under the direction of competent leadership is the best growing Christian. Knowledge is not the enemy of the believer; knowledge is power. And an ignorant believer is the tool of the devil. The devil delights in a believer who is ignorant about the Word of God, because the devil knows that such a believer will not help the church grow and will in fact often be a hindrance to the work of the church. And ignorance has nothing to do with formal education. Some of the most ignorant people I know have a college education. Ignorance is not knowing and not trying to know. Ignorance is thinking that we know it all and refusing to be open to new things. Ignorance is having a closed mind and not being willing to grow. Ignorance is not taking advantage of opportunities to know and grow. I shudder to think how many souls have been turned away from the Lord and the church because of ignorance, because people espoused or received a bunch of half-truths and wrong teachings that could have been corrected if the person had spent less time on the phone gossiping and more time studying the Word of God.

"But grow in the grace and knowledge of our Lord and Savior Jesus Christ. . . ." We grow when we receive knowledge of Jesus Christ through the study the Word of God under the guidance of a body of Christ called "church," which is under the leadership, teaching, and authority of a prepared shepherd who is called by God. Since I have stressed the importance of the flock and the shepherd that we affiliate with, let me again remind us of some of the things this flock under this shepherd believes. We believe in one God infinite and eternal, omniscient, and omnipotent, who has been manifested and revealed in Jesus Christ and who lives among us as the Holy Spirit. We believe that God loves each and every one of us, that God answers prayers, and that God responds to our pleas. We believe that Jesus Christ is the final and fullest revelation of God and that he is both fully human and fully divine. We believe that Jesus came into the world to save sinners and that having conquered death he now reigns as Lord of history. We believe that Jesus died for our sins not because he had to, but because he loves us, and that we matter—truly matter—to him. We believe that the Holy Spirit fills, anoints, and empowers us for service, and that once we have received the Holy Spirit, the Holy Spirit becomes a permanent presence in our lives. We believe that the Bible is the inspired Word of God, written by fallible men and women who were under the inspiration of the Holy Spirit, and that it contains all things necessary for salvation. As 2 Timothy 3:16-17 reminds us, "All scripture is inspired by God and is useful for teaching, for reproof, for correction, and for training in righteousness, so that everyone who belongs to God may be proficient, equipped for every good work."

We believe that the Lordship of Jesus Christ mandates that we give a minimum of ten percent of our time, talent, and money to the church, and that not to tithe is to be in flagrant disobedience to the Word of God. We believe in the one church established by Jesus, which is called by many names and manifested in many traditions. We believe that the church is not simply a haven for saints but a hospital for sinners, that anyone can be saved and that no one is predestined to hell. We believe that anyone and everyone can become new in Christ Jesus. Because we believe in human beings, and because God has been so good to us, as the church we believe that we have a responsibility to reach out and serve others. As the redeemed people of God called "church," we believe that we are called to witness to others and to introduce them to the Jesus who saved us. We believe that because of Jesus' resurrection from the dead we too shall live eternally in a body that is immortal and incorruptible. We believe that according to his Word and promise, Jesus is coming back again in glory, and we shall live with him forever. Until that time, we believe that God wants us to grow and grow and keep on growing.

If you would like to grow, I'd like to introduce you to my friend and elder brother, my Lord and my Savior, Jesus Christ. He will help you to grow from bondage to breakthrough to boldness to bounty. He will help you to grow from being conquered to commitment to courage to a cross to a crown. He will help you to grow from emptiness to excellence to endurance to eternity. He will help you to grow from sin to salvation to sainthood to strength to sanctification.

True Growth Takes Time

TEXT: ACTS 19:8-10

A SMALL INCIDENT I shall never forget—one that taught me a lesson—took place about twenty years ago at a church banquet. I was a pastor in New York at the time, and it was winter. This was before a number of advances in agricultural technology. I was in the buffet line when I spotted a platter of watermelon. As I reached for the watermelon, I asked the minister next to me if he was going to get some. He shook his head. When I asked him why, he said, "Watley, you are a city boy and don't know any better. Those of us who are from the country know this is not the season for watermelons. Any time you see fresh watermelon this time of the year, something is wrong. Something has been added to it or it has been forced to grow."

The enduring lesson is that things can be forced to grow out of their proper season and time. They can be forced to grow too early and too fast. Isn't that what is wrong with a number of our young people? They have been forced to grow out of their proper season. They have been forced to grow up too early and too fast. We have exposed them to too much too soon. We have handed over too much responsibility too early. We have allowed them to make too many decisions about their activities and about what they will and will not do while they are living under our roofs. The result is that they have grown up with adult bodies and technologically adept minds, but their perspectives are warped, their values are twisted, and their attitudes are to be found wanting. Many of our young people have been forced to make adult decisions, wrestle with adult issues, and handle adult responsibilities without having *first* been children.

And much of the blame for their condition lies at the doorsteps of those of us who are supposed to be parents or guardians or adult role models and guides. We have been so busy trying to preserve our own fading youth and doing our own thing that we have failed to be good examples of Christian adulthood and spiritual maturity to our young people. We have been too free in what we have talked about and about whom we have talked in front of them. We have done too much in front of them.

Consequently, when we try to correct them, the first thing they do is throw what they have heard us say and what they have seen us do in our faces. We cannot talk down about the preacher, the church, and our fellow church members in front of our children and then expect the children to respect the church. When they come of age to make their own decisions, they will question whether or not they will attend. We cannot do any and every thing in front of our children and then expect them to listen to us when we try to correct them. Before the streets can get to them, before they leave for their first day of school, children begin to learn and internalize the attitudes, the conduct, and the spirit of the home. Our children can pick their own friends and buddies. They need us to be parents, grandparents, Godparents, guardians, foster parents, uncles, aunts, and saints.

Isn't that what has happened to some of our relationships? We grew them too fast and too soon. We were so needy, we were so loved-starved, and we wanted to get away from where we were so badly, that we consummated a relationship in bed or in marriage too soon and too fast. We were so desperate to settle down and to prove that we could land somebody and relieve the pressure from family and others who were constantly asking us when we were going to get married and have children that we rushed to the altar too soon and too fast. We felt the clock ticking and thought it was now or never. Our fear of being lonely got the best of us, or we felt that we needed somebody to affirm us, or our hormones got the best of us. So we pushed the relationship before true growth and development set in. Or we liked the way the package looked—the credentials were right, the salary was right, the looks were right, the security looked right, the conversation was right, so even though something on the inside was telling us to go slow, we paid our inner voice no attention and rushed full steam ahead too fast and too soon so this good-looking package would not get away from us. Or marriage was a good career move or we were so grateful that somebody looked our way that we grew the relationship too fast and too soon.

The result has been that we have been living with regret and in misery ever since. We became lovers or at least bed partners before we became friends. We were so busy building a relationship that we forgot to build a friendship. We fell in love before we fell in like. It's not enough to simply love somebody. If they are going to share our heart and our life, we need to like them as well. We loved before we learned. We had better take the time to learn a person before we love him or her. We became involved before we became informed. We exposed too much before we became enlightened. We started making plans before we had time to work out our problems. We listened to others instead of listening to ourselves. Or we were so busy being in love with the idea of love or the idea of marriage that we forgot to ask ourselves if we really loved and liked the person we were marrying.

Isn't that what happened to our religion? We grew it too fast and too soon. We became too involved in the politics of the church too fast and too soon. Instead of joining a church and becoming grounded in the Word, we started trying to build a name for ourselves and to establish our identity as a church leader. The result has been that we have become good solid church persons who have the form of godliness, but not the power thereof. We have positions, but no power; we have authority, but no anointing.

We overheard too much gossip and negative conversation too fast and too soon. We know other people's business and dirt, but we know little about the deep things of the Spirit. That is why, in spite of church attendance and involvement, our own personal business, our homes, and our relationships are in turmoil. And we are restless and frustrated.

Or we became too righteous and holy too soon, and now everybody is wrong but us. That is why people look at us and tell us that they liked us better before we got so much religion. I know some people who were fun to be around before they became so deep in the Lord. They smiled more and had more joy. They were happier and knew how to laugh at a joke; they did not take themselves so seriously; they were a pleasure to be around. They were open to suggestions and correction. Now that they are so into the Word and Spirit-filled, they have the personality of Attila the Hun. Their noses are always turned up, their lips are always half poked out, and they are always uptight. They always look better going than they do coming. When they come around, you inhale with caution and reserve, and when they leave, you exhale with relief. They are too serious to really be happy, and they never know how to talk about anything other than the Bible. Every other word out of their mouths is "Jesus," "Hallelujah," or "Praise the Lord." Their conversation and their dress match their personalities, all of which are dull. You can never tell them anything because they are always being instructed and led by the Spirit.

Some of us became too excited with emotion or with the Holy Spirit without being grounded in the Word or in sound teaching; we were easily swayed by every wind and doctrine. Maturity as a follower of Jesus Christ—like the emotional development and maturity of a child and like human relationships—takes time.

Today's text demonstrates the truth that growth, *true growth*, is not an overnight event, but a long-term affair. True growth takes time. When Paul arrived in Ephesus he found two things. First, he found a city that was known for its paganism. On one hand, Ephesus was considered to be the wealthiest and greatest city in the province of Asia. Its commerce and economy established its reputation as the "Vanity Fair" of the Ancient World. On the other hand, Ephesus was also the center for the worship of Artemis or Diana.

The Temple to Artemis, located in Ephesus, was considered one of the seven wonders of the ancient world. This pagan temple was a source of crime and immorality. The temple area held the right of asylum. That meant any criminal who had commited any crime was free if he could reach it. Further, hundreds of priestesses, who were sacred prostitutes, attached themselves to the temple. Ephesus was also known for its famous amulets and charms called Ephesian Letters that were believed to have mysterious powers to heal all kinds of sickness and disease. These charms were supposed to bring children to those who could not have them and ensure success in any contest or journey or undertaking. People came from all over the ancient world to buy them.

In addition to a strong, sinful secular environment, Paul found a weak church. The weakness of this church was evident by the answer they gave when Paul asked a particular question. He asked them if they had received the Holy Spirit when they first believed. They answered that they had not even heard there was a Holy Spirit. They had been baptized into John's baptism, which was one of repentance, but they had not been baptized in the name of Jesus, which meant being ushered into the experience of rebirth.

Paul then baptized them in the name of Jesus. As a sign of the release, outpouring, anointing, and infilling of the Holy Spirit upon and within their lives, they spoke in tongues and prophesied. Altogether there were about twelve believers. Paul began to teach and preach Jesus Christ as Savior and Lord. First, he taught and lectured in the local synagogue, and, after about three months, he moved to a local lecture hall. "This continued for two years, so that all the residents of Asia, both Jews and Greeks, heard the word of the Lord." When one looks at the strength of the Temple of Artemis and the paganism of Ephesus and the weakness of the church, Ephesus seemed like unpromising soil for the seed of Christianity to take root. Yet not only did a solid lasting body of believers emerge in Ephesus, but Ephesus became a gateway for the gospel to be carried to other places in the region.

We can never judge the potential of something or someone by looking at the outside. We can never write off a life or a territory as hopeless ground for change or for the power of the gospel to take root. What may appear unpromising and hopeless to human eyes has potential in God's eyes. For years, people looked at a young flamboyant, carousing, woman-chasing young man and said he would never be anything but a waste. But one day this young man fell under the power of the gospel and the name of Jesus, and, in time, he emerged as St. Augustine, the great African church father. For years people saw John Newton making his living from the African slave trade and said that he was hopelessly lost. But one day John Newton fell under the power of the gospel and the name of Jesus, and, in time, he wrote his testimony, which has become one of the most famous and best loved hymns of the faith:

Amazing grace how sweet the sound, That saved a wretch like me!
I once was lost, but now am found, Was blind, but now I see.

Somebody here, under the sound of my voice, can testify that they too were one of those who others looked at and said were unpromising and without hope. Somebody knows what it is to have others look at their background or their race or their sex or their mistakes or their past and say that they will never amount to much. But thanks be to God, one day some of us fell under the power of the gospel and the name of Jesus. We believed the message that God loves us, Jesus saves to the utmost, and the Holy Spirit will sanctify us and make us brand new. We are witnesses that God will bring forth treasure from what others considered to be trash. God can bring forth nobility from what others thought was nothing. God can bring forth excellence from what others thought was empty.

Paul did a mighty work in Ephesus, but he did not do it overnight. He stayed in Ephesus for two years, which was longer than he stayed anywhere else in his ministry. True growth takes time. It is not an overnight process. This is a truth that we would do well to remember because some times we want God to work instantly. I have seen people come to church because they need to make a change in their lives or they need a job or they are in trouble. They are very faithful and dutiful in attending for about two or three months. But if their situation has not changed in that time, they get disgusted and leave the church and give up on religion, prayer, and God, saying that these things don't work. We forget that it takes time to grow out of some of the situations we have gotten ourselves into. We will give the devil twenty years of our lives and then want God to straighten us out in two weeks. And if God does not take care of our situation, on our timetable, then we go back to the devil we have been serving all of our lives, the same one who got us into our messes to begin with. We will say, "I tried religion, I tried prayer, I tried God, I tried the church, and they didn't do nothing for me."

Well how long did we try them? Did we try the Lord as long as we tried the bottle? Did we try God as long as we tried that crowd we have been hanging out with and the people we have been listening to? Did we try God as long we tried our own schemes and devices? Did we try God—did we try tithing—as long as we tried the numbers, the lottery, the Pick-It, and the slots? Did we try God as long as we tried lying to ourselves and to others? Did we try God as long as we tried overeating, smoking, caffeine, pill popping, casual sex, or any of the other things that we use as stress relievers and coping mechanisms?

And did we really try God? Often when we claim that we are giving God a chance, we are still playing footsy with the devil. Often when we claim we are giving God a chance we are still hanging out with the same deadbeat, dead-end people, going to the same destructive places, flirting with the same addictive temptations, and talking the same negative trash. And then when we don't get delivered, we blame God. Well if you want God to deliver you, you need to give God a little help. Do what you are supposed to do and can do with faithfulness and with your whole heart and give God's work, promises, healing, restoration, and re-*creation* some time.

It took time to dig the hole we are in; it will take time to dig our way out. It took time for us to become so messed up in the head; it will take time for us to get our head straightened out again. It took time for us to get bound or addicted; it will take time for us to become free. It took time for us to become such great liars; it will take time for us to learn to tell the truth as a way of life. (Notice that I said it would take time to develop a lifestyle of truth telling. Even the devil will tell the truth sometimes, but the devil cannot tell the truth as a way of life.) It took time for us to develop bad eating habits; it will take time for us to develop new tastes in food and new eating habits. It took time to become addicted to nicotine and caffeine; it will take time to become smoke-free and caffeine-free. It took time for us to become co-dependent and victims; it will take time for us to develop self-confidence and self-esteem. It took time for us to become negative; it will take time for us to become positive. It took time for us to develop the personalities that we have; it will take time for us to become a new creation. It took time for us to become wounded and for that wound to settle into our spirit; it will take time for us to get over our wounds if that is what we want to do.

Some of us don't want to get over our hurt. We enjoy disliking certain people. We enjoy being martyrs. We enjoy our pity parties and our "woe is me" sessions. We enjoy showing our wounds, parading our hurts, and talking about how we have been wronged. It took time for our relationships to get in the shape they are in. It will take time to rebuild them if we want them rebuilt.

A patch job is instant, but new construction takes time. A repair job can be done right away, but renovation takes time. A bandage can be applied right now, but surgery, which gets to the root of the problem—either by removing or replacing something—takes time. And after the surgery, the healing and the restoration of the body take even more time. True growth takes time and it takes patience. After all, God was patient with us when we were doing everything we thought we were big enough to do. God was patient with us when we were offending his righteousness and holiness with our sin and our shortcomings. God was patient with us when we were hurting his heart, when we were living so far beneath our potential. God was patient with us when we were giving the devil so much of our time and attention. God was patient with us when we were robbing God in tithes and offerings. God was patient with us when we were making wild promises and vows that God knew we were not going to keep. God was patient with us when we were calling on God when trouble came and then going on our merry way once we were delivered. God was patient with us when we were deciding whether or not we were going to give God the opportunity to save us. God has never stopped loving us. God has never stopped believing is us. God has never stopped blessing us. God has never stopped providing for us.

Since God has been so patient with us, why can't we show patience with ourselves and with the time that God's will and Word take to be fulfilled in our lives? Someone may ask why growth and deliverance take so much time and patience other than the fact that what takes time to get into also takes time to get out of. True growth requires time and patience because of the enemy who wars against our growth. As I have said before, the devil does not give up control without a fight. It takes time to grow when the enemy is fighting against us every step of the way. It takes time for us to really understand that we really can defeat the enemy. It takes time to learn the tricks and traps of the enemy. It takes time to recognize the enemy, who disguises himself as a friend and as good.

Why do we fall so easily to the enemy? The enemy does not come to us as an enemy, but as our friend. The enemy comes to us as pleasure. The enemy comes to us as fun. The enemy comes to us as relief. The enemy comes to us as gain without pain and as rewards without sacrifice. The enemy comes to us as the easy way and the short cut. The enemy comes to us as something for nothing and as much for little. The enemy comes to us with immediate gratification. The enemy tells us that we can have what we want right now. Where God deals in truth, the enemy has no problem lying and deceiving us to keep us bound. It takes time to find out that a lie is a lie and the truth is the truth.

When we are dealing with an enemy like the devil, we will make mistakes. There will be times when we will believe the devil's lies over God's truth. There will be times when we will get weak and impatient and go for the quick fix. There will be times when we will tire of the discipline and the commitment that are necessary to reach all that God has for us. There will be times when the vision will seem impossible to reach, and we will be tempted by the enemy to settle for the less that is readily at hand. There will be times when the enemy will use others to get next to us. There will be times when the pressure to conform and be acceptable will be overwhelming. And we will make mistakes. We will stumble along the way. We will backslide. We will take one step forward and two steps back. And every time we fail, we will wonder if we ought to get up and try again. Every failure will be a blow to our self-confidence and self-esteem. Every time we fail, we will discover a weakness or a flaw that has led to our failure. Every time we fail means we will lose time and energy in reaching our goal.

Recovering from our mistakes takes time. Learning from our errors takes time. Recouping our losses takes time. Getting back the ground we lost takes time. Believing in ourselves after we have failed takes time. Our growth takes time, not because God is slow. And it's not because we are weak. In fact, one of the greatest lies the devil tells us is that we are weak and can't do any better than what we are doing. The devil's goal is to make us believe that we have to stay bound or that we cannot grow to the vision that God has for our lives. But we are not weak. Remember that God has a vision for our lives that is greater than any vision we can think of. But if the enemy can shake our confidence in ourselves to reach God's vision or shake our faith in God to bring the vision, then the enemy has won.

Growth takes time and patience because the enemy is such a manipulating, deceiving, and powerful opponent. However, we must remember that as powerful as the enemy is, he is no match for our God. As manipulative and deceiving as the enemy is, he is not smarter than our Savior.

True growth requires time and patience, not because what has taken time to get into takes time to get out of, and not simply because of the enemy who wars against us. True growth requires time and patience because God does not rush when it comes to making quality. God is not in the fast food business. God is not a short order cook. God is a gourmet chef who takes his time to plan and prepare his meal. I once went to a fancy restaurant, and after placing my order the waiter told me that they were featuring a chocolate soufflé for dessert and asked if I wanted to order it. I told him that I wanted to eat my meal first before I ordered my dessert. He told me that was fine for all of the other desserts, but since the soufflés were individually prepared, the chef needed time to prepare them. So if I wanted a soufflé, I had to order it then.

Every life that God develops is individually prepared according to heavenly standards and tastes. And it takes time to develop the quality that God envisions for all of our lives. It took time to make Israel—the spiritual prince who had enough perseverance to wrestle with an angel until his blessing came—from Jacob, thief that he was. It took time to make Moses—the giver of the law from God and leader of God's people to freedom—from the murderer who spoke with a stammering tongue that he was. It took time to make Simon Peter, the preacher, from the cursing fisherman that he was. It took time to make Mary Magdalene, faithful heroine of the Gospels, from a woman who was totally possessed by demons of despondency and depression that she was.

It took time to make Paul, the apostle to the Gentiles, from Saul, the narrow-minded religious bigot that he was. It took time to make the Savior of the world from a baby that was born in a manger in Bethlehem. It took thirty-three years of being tested and tempted by the devil, yet remaining without sin. It took time to develop character that would not compromise even though his disciples left him. It took time to develop faith that was not afraid of either the cross or the grave. It took time for Jesus to conquer death once and for all. He didn't just die and then wake up and jump down from the cross. He was buried in a borrowed tomb, and he stayed in that grave all day and all night, then all day Saturday. Then early Sunday morning he rose to declare that he was alive forevermore and that he had the keys to hell and death in his hands.

The good news that I bring is that if you give Jesus a chance, he will do for you what he has done for so many others. If you want to order a quality life that has anointing and achievement, power and peace, victory and virtue, joy and justice, determination and discipline, excellence and expectation, love and life, forgiveness and faithfulness, courage and commitment, then you can place your order right now because it is going to take time for God to grow you and prepare you. Salvation and Christian living are not simply momentary highs and emotional moments. They are for the long haul. They are about making lifelong commitments. Growth and maturity as a follower of Jesus Christ is a lifelong journey. I am just a waiter with instructions from heaven to take orders for quality living. If you desire to be a quality person, a quality man, a quality woman, a quality parent, a quality spouse, a quality friend, then place your order now. The chef is waiting.

Keep Your Eye on the Grower

TEXT: 1 CORINTHIANS 1:10-13, 3:5-9

IF WE ARE TO GROW to our maximum as children of God, we must keep our eye on the grower. We must keep our eye on the grower, not the foreman. That was one of the mistakes the members of the church in Corinth made in the text. The church in Corinth had been blessed by three of the Lord's very powerful foremen who had supervised the planting of the faith in that city. Corinth was the kind of city—and its membership was the kind of church—that needed strong leadership. As a seaport city, Corinth was one of the most popular harbors of the ancient world. It was constantly being bombarded with all kinds of political, cultural, economic, and religious influences as sailors from all over the ancient world stopped there. Ancient cities that were seaports usually had some kind of nightlife for the sailors who had been at sea for long periods of time and who were looking for relaxation and pleasure when they landed. Corinth was known for its huge temple, built upon a high hill to honor the pagan goddess Aphrodite, in which it is said that 1,000 sacred prostitutes served the constituents who came there to enjoy sexual pleasures under the guise of worship. It is said that at night these prostitutes would come streaming down from the hill where they resided to invade the town, making themselves available to the sailors and anyone else who had come ashore.

Corinth was known for its beautiful women and its sexual looseness. I have been to Corinth. As I stood among its ruins I could just imagine how centuries ago the place where I stood had been alive and booming with the lewdness and immorality of the sex industry that cloaked itself in the garments of worship to a pagan goddess.

One would expect, based on the environment and the context from which they came and in which they had grown up, that persons who came from this community and who made up the church would have a number of issues to work through. In 1 Corinthians 6: 9-11 we get a profile of some of the members of this early church when Paul wrote:

> Do you not know that wrongdoers will not inherit the kingdom of God? Do not be deceived! Fornicators, idolaters, adulterers, male prostitutes, sodomites, thieves, the greedy, drunkards, revilers, robbers—none of these will inherit the kingdom of God. And this is what some of you used to be. But you were washed, you were sanctified, you were justified in the name of the Lord Jesus Christ and in the Spirit of God.

When one reads Paul's letters to the church in Corinth, it seems that it was truly a church with a number of problems. Well when we consider the situation in which they found themselves and the backgrounds of many of its members, we can understand why the church at Corinth had so many internal difficulties. And if the problems in the church at Corinth sound like so many of the problems found in so many of the churches we know, perhaps we are closer to the ancient Corinthians than we realize. The fact that Christianity became firmly established there is again a tribute to the power of the gospel and the work of the Holy Spirit. How could a faith that worshipped a God that could not be seen and had a strict moral, ethical, and sexual code compete with a religion that not only condoned sexual looseness and pleasure but considered such to be an act of worship to a pagan goddess whose temple established a visible presence in the city? How could Peter, Apollos, and Paul compete with 1,000 beautiful sacred prostitutes? Yet Christianity did establish a major beachhead in this war zone of iniquity.

If Christianity could be established and grow in Corinth, it can grow anywhere. If the gospel could turn around the lives of the people of Corinth, it can turn anybody's life around. Logic says that a numerically and financially weak faith and a fledgling religion with a strong moral code would not have found an audience in a hellhole like Corinth. But reality and history say something different. They tell us that even in Corinth, God's Word, God's power, and God's people can have tremendous breakthroughs.

And whenever we begin to question how large and how strong our church can become in the place where we are, we need to think about the church in Corinth. Whenever we begin to question the power of the gospel to change lives, we need to think about the church in Corinth. And whenever we begin to feel overwhelmed because of the challenges and the obstacles that would stunt or thwart our growth, we need to think about the church in Corinth. Whenever we begin to feel discouraged that we are not growing or our situation is not growing or those whose lives we are trying to touch do not seem to be changing for the better, we need to think about the church in Corinth and know that if God could do something in Corinth, God can do something in our situation. If God could turn around the lives of the people of Corinth, God can do it again. The gospel can do it again; the blood of Jesus can do it again; the Holy Spirit can do it again in our lives, as well as the lives of those for whom we pray. Whenever we become discouraged and begin to doubt, we need to think about Corinth and pray, "If you did it there, I know that you can do it here. You are that same Lord whose power is unlimited and who always has mercy. You did it yesterday. Do it again today, right now, right here—with me, with us, with my children, with my parents, with my sisters and brothers, with my family, with my loved ones. You moved by your power and spirit divine long ago in Corinth; move right now, right here I pray in the name of the same Jesus that turned the lives of the Corinthians around. Work a miracle in me and in my situation."

God was able to do such a mighty work in Corinth because of three powerful representatives—Peter, Apollos, and Paul, each of whom had ministered there at one time or another. Let us never forget that God never accomplishes the work of healing, of growth, of salvation in a vacuum. God works in and through human instruments. If we want God to do a mighty work in our lives, then we must give God some help. We must do our part. Don't ask God to heal us when we don't do our part—when we don't watch our diet, when we don't exercise, when we continue to smoke and drink, when we don't get the proper rest. Don't ask God to deliver us from temptation when we keep going around the things and the people for which we have a weakness. If you don't want the lion to bite you, don't keep putting your head in the lion's mouth. If you don't want the fire to burn you, quit playing with matches. Don't ask the Lord to give us a financial blessing or to straighten out our finances when we don't do our part—when we don't tithe, when we continue to buy simply because we see, without any effort to change our lifestyle or spending habits.

God did not descend from heaven and break up the fallow ground in Corinth and stand on the street corner and preach to himself. God reached the people of Corinth through his human instruments. We must never underestimate our role in church growth. The church cannot grow unless we help it to grow. The church cannot grow unless we invite people to come to our church so that they can receive the good news of salvation, the presence of the living Christ, and the anointing of the Holy Spirit that makes growth possible and without which growth does not happen.

How blessed the church at Corinth was to have strong leaders like Peter, who was the first among the disciples to confess Jesus as the Son of the Living God. It was upon the rock of his confession of faith that the Church of Christ was founded. How blessed the church in Corinth was to have a strong, eloquent, spellbinding preacher like the African, Apollos. For Apollos was from Alexandria, Egypt. Thus the church in Corinth was partly evangelized and developed by an African. How blessed the church of Corinth was to have come under the teaching and nurture of the powerful and effective apostle Paul. Of course, when one considers the contexts and background, strong leadership was needed.

The strongholds of Satan will not fall without strong leadership.

If Satan has built major fortresses in our lives or in the lives of our loved ones or in the life of our community, those fortresses will not fall by our wishing them to fall or pleading and whining and begging in prayer that they fall. Those of us who are the people of God must learn how to walk in boldness in bringing them down. We must pray boldly. We must witness boldly. We must speak the truth with boldness. We must live what we believe with boldness. We must give with boldness because we know that God is so good and God has always taken care of us and God always will. We must take the initiative in challenging the rule and reign of Satan in our lives. We must tell Satan that he cannot have our lives or the lives of those we love. We must claim our families and our lives, our churches and our communities for Christ. We must not be afraid of the powers that oppose us. We must really know that greater is the power that is within us than any power that is within the world. When we are engaged in spiritual warfare, the timid soldier will be overrun and defeated. Our families and lives will not be saved without strong leadership on our part. Demons will not be uprooted in our lives or the lives of those around us without strong leadership on our part. Our communities will not be reclaimed without strong leadership on our part. Let the redeemed of the Lord not ask so, or wish so, but say so.

Although the strong leadership of Peter, Apollos, and Paul had blessed the church in Corinth, their blessing had become a source of division and factionalism among them. Let me just hastily warn us about allowing Satan to turn our blessings into problems. Satan specializes in turning the blessings of God into hindrances to our growth and development. The money that is a blessing can become a hindrance when we start becoming more devoted to it than to growing. I imagine that there is not a person here who feels that they love money more than they love God. But if you don't love your money more than you do God, then why don't you tithe? If you don't love your money more than you do God, why are you so joyless and grudging and stingy and cheap in your giving? If you don't love your money more than you do God, then why do you get upset when I start talking about you giving more of it?

The job that God has blessed us with can become a hindrance when we become so devoted to it that we neglect our families, our relationships, and our tithe of time to the Lord in order to do more work. That job can become a hindrance to our growth when we become so tired that we don't have time to devote to the Lord. And if you don't think that that job is a blessing, ask somebody who doesn't have one and who needs one. That relationship that God has blessed us to have can become a hindrance when we become so devoted to it that we stop coming to church or cut back on our church activities so that we can develop that relationship. God was with you before that person came into your life and when that person is no longer there, and God will still be with you. You don't neglect God for anyone. Instead, like Solomon did with the Queen of Sheba, you bring them with you to the house of the Lord so that they can see the source of your blessings. Anyone whom you have to neglect God for is not the person for you. You had better take a second look at anyone who does not respect your faith and does not support your involvement and participation in the church. Be careful about becoming involved with anyone who refuses to come to church with you. If they don't come now when you are single, what makes you think that they are going to change once you get married and they don't have to impress you anymore? Don't allow that house or that car that you have been blessed with to become a hindrance to your growth because you are staying away from church on Sunday morning to clean or care for it. The Lord's Day is for the worship of the Lord, not for house cleaning or car caressing.

Don't allow the education that God has blessed you with to become a hindrance to your praise. You don't know what your degrees mean. The B.A. means Born Again, and the second birth is something to praise God for. The B.S. means Battling Still. I may have made some mistake but I'm not giving up. I'm battling still and that's something to praise God for. The M.A. means More Anointing. And that's something to praise God for. The M.S. means My Salvation. And that's something to praise God for. The M.F.A. means My First Ambition is to glorify God, who gives growth. The M.D. means More Delights. When we keep our eye on the grower, he has more delights for us. The J.D. means Joy Divine: what a fellowship, what a joy divine, leaning on the everlasting arms. And that's something to praise God for. The M.S.W. means My Savior's Wonderful. When we realize how wonderful Jesus is, that's something to praise God for. And the Ph.D. means Prayer Handles Demons. And knowing that through prayer you have victory over demons is something to praise God for. No matter what degree we have, it ought to focus us on the Grower. I repeat, don't allow any of the blessings that God sends into your lives cause you to take your eye off the Blesser. As James 1:17 reminds us, "Every generous act of giving, with every perfect gift, is from above, coming down from the Father of lights, with whom there is no variation or shadow due to change."

The church in Corinth had been blessed at different times by three of the strongest leaders in the early church. However, what started out as a blessing had become a hindrance to the Corinthians' growth because they took their eye off of the Grower who had put them there and began to focus instead on their feeling and loyalties to their favorite pastor or leader. Now it is appropriate to honor and give thanks for our spiritual leaders. The Bible tells us that the elders who rule well are worthy of double honor. When we go to a restaurant, a chef who prepares delicious food is deserving of our thanks and praise. Often when we say grace we give thanks not only for the food but also for the hands that prepared it. However, we don't become so carried away with the preparations of the chef that we forget that unless a chef has something to cook he cannot do anything. We are nourished not by the chef but by the food that the Grower provides. If the Grower hadn't provided the food first, then the chef would have nothing to cook. And all chefs are dependent upon the same Grower. So while we are grateful to the chefs for the role they play in making food palatable and enjoyable, we don't focus so much on the chefs that we take our eyes off of the Grower.

That was the point Paul was making when he wrote the words of the text and said:

Now I appeal to you, brothers and sisters, by the name of our

> Lord Jesus Christ, that all of you be in agreement and that there be no divisions among you, but that you be united in the same mind and the same purpose.... What I mean is that each of you says, "I belong to Paul," or "I belong to Apollos," or "I belong to Cephas," or "I belong to Christ." Has Christ been divided? Was Paul crucified for you? Or were you baptized in the name of Paul?
>
> What then is Apollos? What is Paul? Servants through whom you came to believe, as the Lord assigned to each. I planted, Apollos watered, but God gave the growth. So neither the one who plants nor the one who waters is anything, but only God who gives the growth.

This Word is still relevant because some of us today still base our commitment and service to the Grower upon how we feel about the foremen that are over the vineyards. Some persons are not in church today because they took their eyes off of the Grower and placed them on the foremen. It is the Grower who wakes them up every day and starts them on their way. It is the Grower who answers their prayers and makes ways out of no ways for them. It is the Grower who saved them through the precious blood of his only Son, Jesus Christ. It is the Grower who sent the Holy Spirit to empower them in their weakness, comfort them in their sorrow, and to lead them into all truth. It is the Grower who healed them when they were sick. And when they were in trouble it was the Grower that they promised, if they were delivered, to serve with everything they had. Yet because they have certain disagreements with certain foremen, they stop serving the Grower. No matter how we feel about certain foremen, keep your eyes on the Grower, because he is the one we are supposed to be serving. We honor the foremen, but we keep our eyes on the Grower.

Keep your eye on the Grower, not on other seeds that are growing along with us. Some of us cannot grow to our maximum because we are so busy looking at other seeds that have been planted in the garden. We can't grow because we are so busy watching what other seeds have that we don't have. We can't grow because we are so busy disliking other seeds, being jealous and trying to hold back other seeds to keep them from outgrowing us. We can't grow to our maximum because we are angry with God, because other seeds seem to have more than we have. However, nobody ever reaches his or her peak when he or she lives life trying to compete with somebody else. We grow to our capacity only when we ask the Grower to grow us to the fullest. We grow to the fullest only when we ask the Grower to stir up our gifts and to grow our gifts. So keep your eye on the Grower, because only the Grower has a vision for our lives and only the Grower can grow us to our maximum. Instead of spending our time watching the growth of other seeds, we ought to be seeking the Grower for a vision for our lives.

Keep your eye on the Grower and not on yourself. When we keep our eyes on ourselves, we are limited by our assessment and our failure to understand that we have more resources than we can see with the naked eye. Isn't that the enduring lesson of the prophet Elisha at Dothan? When we keep our eyes on ourselves, all we can see is our limitations. When we keep our eyes on ourselves, all we can feel is overwhelmed and frightened, justifiably so when we see the mountains that must be climbed, the opposition that must be faced, the burdens that must be borne, and the hurdles and obstacles that must be overcome. But when we keep our eye on the Grower, then, like Isaiah, we know that no weapon formed against us shall prosper. When we keep our eye on the Grower we understand that "those who wait for the LORD shall renew their strength, they shall mount up with wings like eagles, they shall run and not be weary, they shall walk and not faint" (Isaiah 40:31). When we keep our eye on the Grower we understand, like Paul, that we can do all things through Christ who strengthens us (Philippians 4:13). When we keep our eye on the Grower, then we understand that we have a power at work within us that can do more abundantly than what we can ask or imagine to the glory of Christ. When we keep our eye on the Grower, we understand that the weapons of our warfare are not merely human, but they have divine power to destroy strongholds.

Keep your eye on the Grower and not on the weeds growing along with you in the garden. I know that some of us are trying to grow in the midst of weeds. We have weeds in our jobs, weeds in our homes, weeds in our churches, weeds at our tables, weeds in our beds, weeds in our business, weeds everywhere we turn. We have to contend with demonic weeds, discouraging weeds, busybody weeds, tongue-wagging weeds, troublemaking weeds, ignorant weeds, unsaved weeds, no-vision weeds, co-dependent weeds, racist weeds, sexist weeds, alcoholic weeds, drug addict weeds, self-righteous weeds, jealous weeds, fault-finding weeds, super-sensitive-always-getting-feelings-hurt weeds, and petty weeds. Every time we try to grow there is a weed trying to wrap itself around us to keep us from reaching our fullest height. I know that weeds can be a pain to deal with, but keep your eye on the Grower because the Grower also has his eye on the weeds. The Grower is not going to let a weed block out any of the blessings of sunlight that you need to keep growing. Keep your eye on the Grower and know that the Grower will take care of the weeds. That's what David was talking about when he said, "Do not fret because of the wicked; do not be envious of wrongdoers, for they will soon fade like the grass, and wither like the green herb.... Commit your way to the LORD; trust in him, and he will act. He will make your vindication shine like the light, and the justice of your cause like the noonday" (Psalm 37:1-2,5-6).

Keep your eye on the Grower and not on the clouds, looking for the next rainstorm. Some of us can't grow because we are worried about what might happen. But if you keep your eye on the Grower then you know that the Grower is able to grow you through the storms. What if I try to grow and this happens and that happens? I'll tell you what will happen when the unexpected happens—the Grower will take care of you and help you to keep on growing. What if I try and fail? Well, if you keep your eye on the Grower you won't fail because there is no failure in God. Whatever vision God gives to us and plants within our hearts and souls, God is able to bring it to pass. Doubters may discourage and demons may disturb, but God will bring it to pass. Heathens may hinder and hellhounds may holler, but God will bring it to pass. Trials may trouble and burdens may battle, but God will bring it to pass. Enemies may excel sometimes and opposition may plant obstacles, but God will bring it to pass. In God's own way and in God's own time, God will bring it to pass. Oh yes, he will. I know he will.

So keep your eye on the Grower because the Grower gives the vision. We don't give ourselves our own vision, because it would then be no bigger than we are. We don't receive the vision from others, because then the vision of our life would be no bigger than their perception or opinion of us. The originator of the vision for our lives is the Grower. The vision for our salvation came from God. When we were hopelessly bound by sin and death stood as our eternal sentence; when the law that was intended to teach us the right thing ended up condemning us; when the words of prophets fell on deaf ears—God had a vision of divinity wrapping itself up in the garments of humanity and being born a baby whose name would be Jesus, because he would save us form our sins. And when the devil decided to defeat Jesus with a cross, God had a vision of Jesus using that same cross to save a dying humanity. And when evil men decided to seal him in a borrowed tomb, God had another vision of raising him to stoop no more and with all power in his hands. Keep your eye on the Grower because the Grower has the vision for your life.

Then keep your eye on the Grower because only the Grower can grow the vision. That's what Paul was talking about when he wrote, "I planted, Apollos watered, but God gave the growth." When we've done the best we can and our best is not good enough, God's power connects itself to our best and gives the growth anyhow. Through our ups and our downs, God gives the growth. Through our heartache and pain, God gives the growth. Through our feeble praying, God gives the growth. With our half-hearted efforts, God gives the growth. When our strength runs out, God gives the growth. When demons attack, God gives the growth.

God of grace and glory, grow your vision for our lives in us. Jesus Christ, our Savior and Lord, grow your vision for our lives in us. Holy Spirit, our comforter and guide, grow your vision for our lives in us.

Are You Ready for the Next Level?

TEXT: 1 CORINTHIANS 3:1-4

WHEN MY GRANDDAUGHTER Madison Savannah was about twelve weeks old, I once held her while I was eating some garlic shrimp. I happened to look down at her and saw her eyes focused on the shrimp that was on my fork. Her eyes were saying to me, "Grandpa, I am really tired of the formula my mother has been feeding me. I sure would like to taste some of that shrimp you are eating. Would you let me have just a taste of it?" My daughter, Jennifer, must have read my thoughts while I was looking at Madison, because from across the table she spoke up and said, "Dad, don't you dare." But the time is rapidly approaching when her child will make the switch from formula to solid food, and when that time comes it would not be in that child's best maturational interests to keep her on formula. At some point babies must make the switch from formula to solid food. We would think it strange to see a five- or six-year-old walking around still sucking on a bottle. When a child stays on the bottle too long we speak to the mother and tell her that it is time to wean the child, to move that child to the next level of diet so that he or she can continue to grow.

As the spiritual father of the Corinthian church, Paul was concerned with the spirituality of that group of believers. He understood the importance of beginning with the elementary things of the faith, things such as the profound yet easy-to-understand message of God's love and salvation from their sins through the action of God in Jesus Christ. With their confession of faith that Jesus Christ is Lord and Savior, the Corinthian believers had received the anointing and the gifting of the Holy Spirit. But Paul understood that there is more to being a Christian than being saved and rejoicing about one's new life in the Holy Spirit. Learning how to walk in or use the gifts of the Spirit, the development of a spirit of generosity, learning how to witness to others and grow the church all awaited them. Learning how to handle the demons; learning the social, economic, and political implications of the gospel; and learning other mysteries of God awaited them. Receiving the fullness of God awaited them.

Paul was not trying to rush the learning process. He understood the importance of Christian nurture. Paul recognized that new believers who are babes in Christ, like newborn babes in life, can be damaged by being exposed to too much too soon. I need to stress this point over and over again. Instead of nurturing new believers, too many of us seasoned believers are turning them off by exposing them to too much too soon. New believers who have been drawn to Christ because of the ministry of a certain pastor do not need to hear all of your issues and dislikes regarding that pastor, who was an instrument in leading them to the Lord and to the church. New believers do not need to hear the prevailing gossip and talk regarding other saints. New believers do not need to hear some of the underground, unwritten history of the church they just joined and are excited about. And, particularly, new believers do not need to be hit on by some of the needy, sexually frustrated, forward saints.

Jesus once sat a little child in the midst of the disciples and said to them, "If any of you put a stumbling block before one of these little ones who believes in me, it would be better for you if a great millstone were fastened around your neck and you were drowned in the depth of the sea" (Matthew 18:6). The Word of God tells us that we shall give an account for every vain and idle word we speak. And when we as seasoned believers—with our wagging tongues, cynical and negative attitudes, personal issues and vendettas, turf-guarding spirits, and callous and hurting words—cause a new believer or babe in Christ to stumble, I believe we will have to answer for that some day. Some of us will not even have to wait for the final judgment; we will begin to reap judgment and the displeasure of God in this life for our insensitivity regarding the fragile faith and belief systems of new believers.

Paul understood the value of Christian nurture and of not trying to rush or force Christian maturity. However he also recognized that it was detrimental to believers' development to keep them on the basics of the faith for too long. At some point they should be ready to grow to the next level. Thus he wrote, "And so, brothers and sisters, I could not speak to you as spiritual people, but rather as people of the flesh, as infants in Christ. I fed you with milk, not solid food, for you were not ready for solid food. Even now you are still not ready, for you are still of the flesh." Paul was saddened because the Corinthian believers were still not ready to move to the next level of their spiritual development. They were an organized church. They had been blessed by some of the most talented and anointed leadership of the church. Paul, Simon Peter, and the great preacher Apollos had all ministered among them. The gifts of the Holy Spirit were operating in their midst. Yet they were still not ready to go to the next level of their spiritual development.

The Corinthian believers were like my laptop and me. As a number of you know, for about two years I have been typing my sermons and doing much of my work on my laptop. When I first started using my computer I recognized that it had the potential to do so much more than the tasks I was doing on it. Its capacity was far beyond my knowledge of its workings. And I told myself I needed to sit down and learn all of the stuff that my computer could do. Well, it has been over two years since I started using my laptop, and I still have not taken the time to explore all it can do. I still have not learned Power Point. I still have not learned how to fax things with it. While I am computer literate, I still have not moved to the next level in my use and familiarity with the intricacies of my laptop.

That is the way it is with our faith. When we are believers in Jesus there is so much that God wants to do with our lives and bring from our lives. We have capacity that we have not even thought about. That was what Paul was talking about when he wrote to the Ephesians, "Now to him who by the power at work within us is able to accomplish abundantly far more than all we can ask or imagine, to him be glory in the church and in Christ Jesus to all generations, forever and ever. Amen" (Ephesians 3:20-21). Whatever power that was available to believers in the New Testament is also available to us. The Holy Spirit has not lost its power. As believers we have power to heal the sick, raise the dead, and cast out the demons that trouble our lives and hold captive our loved ones. We can do whatever Peter, Paul, Philip, and the other believers did. Jesus promised that greater works than his we could do.

Think about that. We have the potential not only to duplicate the works of Jesus, but to go beyond them. That is how much power and potential salvation in the name of Jesus is bestowed upon us. Yet we as believers are still bound by fear. We continue to fall into the same traps and sins over and over again. We are still afraid to take chances. We still talk about what we cannot do. We still doubt and panic when things get rough and get tight. We still act like Chicken Littles running around saying the sky is falling and everything is going to collapse because we experience a little bump on the head. With all the Lord has brought us through, with over two thousand years of Christian tradition behind us, with all of the prayers that we have seen answered, we are still weak and ineffectual in our prayer life. We still don't know the Word of God. We still are not ready for the next level of our walk with the Lord.

Paul told the Corinthian church that they were still in the flesh. One of the reasons I have not learned more on my laptop is that I have become satisfied and comfortable with the tasks I am able to do on it. While I know that it has capacity for more, what I know about it is enough to do the basic things I need it to do. While we know that we are not perfect, neither are we all that bad. Thus we have become comfortable with where we are.

We have enough religion and faith to meet our basic needs. We have enough religion and faith to give us respectability. We have enough religion and faith to make us feel good. We have enough religion and faith to give us the security of a safety net in the event we get into trouble. We have enough religion and faith to be saved. While we are not all that we could be, we have enough religion to testify that we are not what we used to be. We keep most of the commandments, and since we don't know anyone who keeps all of them, we are content to let the devil get the victory some time. After all, we are only human.

We need to remember the words of Stephen Covey, who in his *Seven Habits of Highly Effective People* said that the enemy of the best is the good. The Corinthian believers were like so many of us: they were good Christians. However Paul wanted them to move beyond good to be the best they could be. What is often cute in a baby has no place in an adult. Baby vision is good for babies. Baby faith is good for babies. Baby prayer is good for babies. Baby praise is good for babies. But at this point in our lives we ought to have a matured faith that takes on mountains. We ought to be moving toward matured vision that sees the impossible and knows that it can be reached because God is on our side. We ought to be moving toward matured prayer that can pray down miracles. We ought to be moving toward matured praise that acknowledges, recognizes, and glorifies God even before the miracle happens and even in difficult times.

The Corinthian Christians were carnal, or in the flesh, because they had become comfortable in being where they were. They were not seeking to go any higher, and they were not seeking to go any deeper. Then they were in the flesh because they had too much of their former attitudes and sins with them. The other day I tried to save something on my computer and could not. For a minute I did not know what was wrong or what to do. Then I remembered that earlier a notice had appeared on the screen telling me that my hard drive was full. A computer has limited capacity, and I had too much stuff stored on it. Before I could save the new document I had to save it onto a diskette. Then I went into my computer and began to delete some of the stuff that was there. When I did so, I was surprised at some of the stuff I had saved that was serving no purpose, but was just taking up needed space.

Before some of us can move to the next level, we are going to delete some of the stuff we have been carrying in our lives. Our hearts, souls, and minds do not have unlimited capacity to store stuff. And if we keep all of those old hurts, all of those old feuds, all of those old fears, all of those old insecurities, all of that old guilt, all of that old jealousy, then there will be no room for God to bring forth something new. There is not enough room for both old jealousy and new joys. There is not enough room for both old attitudes and new anointing. There is not enough room for both old rivalries and fresh revelation. There is not enough room for both old feuds and fresh faith. There is not enough room for both old guilt and new growth. There is not enough room for both old grudges and new gifts. There is not enough room for both old pain and new possibilities. There is not enough room for both old vengeance and new visions.

And if you ever start deleting stuff and receiving something new from the Lord, you will wonder why you held onto some stuff for so long. David asked the Lord to create within him a clean heart and to renew within him a right spirit. However for that to happen, David realized that he had to get rid of some of the stuff he had been carrying. So he asked the Lord to delete it. He said, "Search me, O God, and know my heart; test me and know my thoughts. See if there is any wicked way in me, and lead me in the way everlasting" (Psalm 139:23-24).

The Corinthian church could not go to the next level because of the flesh, which lead to a quarrelsome and divisive spirit. Division is of the devil. We may disagree, but when we have a quarrelsome spirit that causes us to fight each other and becomes so troublesome that it interferes with our worship and the growth and the working of the church, then it is of the devil. When we stay at a certain level it is easy for the devil to get to us. That is why the devil has gotten to some of our families, our finances, our faith, our careers, and our relationships. We have stayed at a level where the devil can easily get to us. However when we move to the next level, the devil may rise against us but will not prevail. When we get to a certain level, certain people can't get to us. Certain things they say don't bother us anymore. We learn how to put them in the hands of the Lord and let the Lord fight the battle. We even learn how to praise God for the victory even before the battle starts.

Somebody here ought to be able to testify, "I can remember a time when if the devil had sent such a trial into my life or if such a person had said or done a certain thing to me, it would have broken my spirit. I would have given up and left the church and turned around from the way in which I was walking. But now that I have grown, things that used to send me home in tears and make me doubt my gifts and calling can't stop me anymore. Now that I have reached a new place in the Lord, I know that even though my feelings get hurt I will get over it and keep on serving the Lord. Even if I get hit hard, I know that I will come through it. Even if I get discouraged, I know that the experience will soon pass and renewal will come. Even if I get knocked down, I know that I will not stay down forever; I will rise again. Even if I can't see my way clearly, I now know that the Lord will make a way somehow. Even if supporters fail me and turn their backs on me, I now know that I have a friend who sticks closer than a brother, who will never leave me or forsake me. And even if I lose some battles I know that the war will still be won."

Then there was another reason the Corinthian church was not ready for the next level. They were cheap. In 2 Corinthians, chapters 8 and 9, Paul talks to them about their cheapness and stinginess. Paul had undertaken a drive to collect an offering from the Gentile churches to assist the mother church in Jerusalem, which had come across some difficult times. Some of the other churches such as the ones in Macedonia had responded generously, but not the Corinthians. You can't get to the next level by being cheap. Non-tithers are under a curse and will not receive the fullness of God's outpouring and blessings. According to the Word of God, those who do not tithe the full tithe—that is the gross—are thieves and robbers. It's in the

Book. And thieves and robbers, even if they are saved, even if they speak in tongues, even if they are leaders and officers, even if they preach the gospel, do not receive the fullness of God's outpouring. The tithe is the key that unlocks the window of heaven and causes the overflow to come into our lives. We can stretch out at the altar all night long. We can say "in the name of Jesus" over and over again. We can have gifts of prophecy and interpretation. But hear this clear word of instruction: unless you tithe consistently, regularly, and faithfully off of your gross—the total yield of your field—you will not get to the next level of growth, power, and blessing.

Are you ready to grow to the next level? I have told you the story that my Daddy used to tell about the pilot who took off on a solo flight. Everything was going well for a while. Then all of a sudden he began to feel himself losing control. Being a believer he asked the Lord what he should do. The Spirit spoke to him and told him to kick open the control panel. The pilot kicked open the control box next to his right foot, and there he saw rats eating at his wires. The rats were so far up in the control panel that he could not reach them. He prayed earnestly about what he should do. The Spirit again told him to point the nose of the plane higher, and give it all the gas he could. The pilot in obedience took the plane higher, and when he reached a certain altitude where the air was less dense, the rats could not breathe, and so they died. Are you tired of rats eating away at your reputation? Rats eating away at your finances? Rats eating away at your relationships? Rats eating away at your family? Rats eating away at your faith? Rats eating away at your joy? Rats eating away at your career and your job? Rats eating away at your dreams and your visions?

I know somebody who can take you to another level where rats may rise but they can't abide. And his name is Jesus. When Lucent Technologies wired a new building that I know about, they gave the owners a twenty-year guarantee on the wiring they had installed. That meant that the wiring would not only last twenty years but also that the wiring had the capacity to handle whatever new technology might be invented over the next twenty years. Well we have a Savior who has an unlimited warranty. He is Savior and he is Lord forever more. The same blood that cleansed two thousand years ago is able to cleanse today. The same love that forgave and gave second chances to those who had messed up is still available now. We also have a Savior who has given us unlimited capacity to handle anything we might face in the future. When you receive him as Lord and Savior, you do not need to fear any future lies that may arise in times to come. You already have the capacity to handle them. You need not fear any future trouble that the devil may inflict because in the Lord Jesus Christ you already have the capacity to handle it. You need not fear any future illness or diseases that may strike your body because in the Lord Jesus Christ you already have the capacity for victory. You need not fear any future rats that may attack, because in the Lord Jesus Christ you already have the capacity to defeat them. You need not fear any future sin into which you may fall because in the Lord Jesus Christ you already have the capacity for cleansing and a fresh start. You need not fear any future traps that the devil may set because in the Lord Jesus Christ you already have the capacity to be delivered.

If you truly receive Jesus as Savior and as Lord, with the Holy Spirit you can reach and attain a new level. You will have joy, unspeakable and full of glory. You will have peace that passes understanding. You will have grace that is sufficient and strength that is made perfect in weakness. You will have the promises of God as your foundation and the power of the Holy Spirit as your battle-axe. And when this life is over and you must lay down and press a dying pillow, you will have the assurance of another building—a house not made with hands, eternal in the heavens. But to get to that level, Jesus has to take you there.

Growing Beyond Your Classification

TEXT: ACTS 6:8-15, 7:54-60

LIKE TRAFFIC, telephones, taxes, and television, classification is a standard feature of life in our culture. We start off life by being classified on our birth certificates by gender and by race. We go through life being classified by age, from infants to toddlers to adolescents to teenagers to young adults to middle age to seniors. And if you don't think accurate records are being kept of your age, just wait until you approach 50 and one day in your mail, without your applying or telling anyone your age, you will receive an application to join the AARP, the American Association of Retired Persons. When I received my application in the mail my first reaction was, "There must be some mistake. I know I am not this old. Retirement has not even crossed my mind. I am still a long way from 65." I was told that you are eligible for membership in AARP as early as age 50. Then I said, "How did these people get my age and my address?" I was told, "I don't know how they do it but they have a way."

In the course of living we face other types of classification, such as fat or skinny, athletic or non-athletic, sick or healthy, homely or good-looking, legitimate or illegitimate (which is a term that is a misnomer, since God does not create illegitimate life). We are often classified by our jobs or careers, whether we are so-called professionals or so-called common laborers. We are classified by education, by intelligence, by socio-economic standing: lower class, middle class, and upper class. Classification is a way of identifying people by certain characteristics. The purpose of classification is informational, not deterministic. Classification is not supposed to put a ceiling on anyone's aspirations or define the parameters of their existence. What often happens, however, is that we use classifications as boxes into which we put people and to tell them what is expected of them and what they can or cannot do. We often treat class like a cast. A cast is a mold into which we pour a fluid or liquid substance, and when that fluid hardens into the shape of the mold, it becomes whatever the mold is. When the substance is liquid or fluid, it can become anything. But once it hardens in a mold, then unless it is melted down again, it remains that thing for as long as it exists.

Sometimes we tell people that because they are classified in certain ways that certain things are permissible and certain things are off limits for them. We like to tell women about where their place is and where it is not. We like to tell people to act their age. We like to tell people with certain backgrounds that they can be expected to go only so far and to do so much and that certain goals are beyond their reach. Racism is a sin that likes to put people into a cast and tell certain people what they can or cannot do based upon their racial or ethnic identity. I have often been in discussions with politicians and others about the state of our society. The conversation went along as expected when we were discussing things like drugs, crime, welfare, and jobs. But when I began to ask questions about the economy or the stock market or the eternal crisis in the Middle East or other international issues, people, including my own, have looked at me as if to say, "What is he asking about that for?" Sometimes we think in terms of ethnic or women's issues and feel that conversations ought to be confined to those concerns. When we step outside of the box and go beyond what is classified as minority or women's issues, people look at us strangely, as if our brain is not supposed to be able to think beyond a certain range of concerns. We cannot stop people from classifying us in their minds and coming up with a set of limitations and expectations for us based upon their classification. However what we *can* control is our buying into and our acceptance of the expectations of others based upon their classification of us. We can grow beyond our classification.

As believers and in the church we also play the classification game. We classify churches as contemporary or traditional. We sometimes forget that the gospel is both contemporary and traditional. It ought to be contemporary enough to speak to our present needs, but it has a 2,000-year tradition behind it of offering salvation to lost souls. We classify churches based upon their name. We sometimes forget that there is but one gospel, and that is the gospel of our Lord and Savior Jesus Christ. And there is but one heaven and one hell. And no matter what churches you belong to, we are all going to end up one place or the other. We pick a church based upon its doctrine, whether it is Christ-centered, Bible-based, and Spirit-filled. We pick a church based upon whether it teaches tithing, because tithing is Bible-based and blessing-filled. I don't believe non-tithing churches receive the fullness of God's blessings because they are robbing God, and churches, like individuals, cannot receive the fullness of God's blessings when they rob God. We pick a church based upon whether it meets our growth, intellectual, and spiritual needs. We should not be picking a church based upon the denominational label or classification.

We classify people as newcomers and as old-timers. We like to talk in terms of how long we have been here and those who just got here. We classify people based upon their giving. We classify people based upon their title, or position, or office. Like the world, we not only classify people, but we sometimes also use those classifications to set limits or expectations of an individual's spirituality, commitment, or involvement. We sometimes say that we don't have members like we used to, as if new members do not have the same commitment to the church as old members of those of bygone days. When new members try to make suggestions or get involved, sometimes persons who are more concerned about their positions treat them with a negative spirit that essentially says, "Who do you think you are making a suggestion or acting like you have a brain? You just got here. Who do you think you are coming in here trying to take over? Who do you think you are offering leadership and becoming involved? That's Miss So and So's job."

As a believer, you cannot afford to let anyone limit your growth and your involvement based upon his or her classification of you. You cannot buy into anyone's classification of your abilities or their perception of your gifts. You can outgrow your classification. Stephen in our text is a case in point. We meet Stephen in Acts 6, when the church had become involved with some stuff that was threatening to break their unity, stifle ministry, and limit growth. The widows who spoke Greek were complaining that they were being neglected and discriminated against in the daily distribution of bread. The Greek-speaking widows accused the Hebrew-speaking widows of receiving more bread and more food than they did. The controversy reached such proportions that the Apostles themselves had to be called in to mediate the situation. The Apostles correctly understood that they could not continue to grow the church to the vision of Christ and be personally involved in the distribution of bread. You cannot grow and become involved in every dogfight and disagreement and controversy that people bring to you. People who dabble in mess, who love small stuff, will keep you mired in it just like they are if you let them. Sometimes we just have to say to people, "I know this is important to you, but I have bigger fish to fry and I am going to devote only so much energy and time to this issue. With all due respect to what you are dealing with, my world is bigger than this issue."

That is what the apostolic council told the church. They said they would not forsake the vision Christ had for their lives; they would not neglect their time with God and their study of the Scriptures in order to count the number of slices of bread everybody was receiving. They told those who were concerned with this issue to select seven persons from among themselves who were individuals of good standing, who were filled with the Holy Spirit, and who with wisdom could oversee the daily distribution of food to those who needed such ministry. Among those who were chosen, Stephen is the first name listed. In Acts 6:5 Stephen is described as "a man full of faith and the Holy Spirit." Acts 6:8 tells us that "Stephen, full of grace and power, did great wonders and signs among the people." In Acts 6:15 we are told that Stephen had the face of an angel. The Bible does not tell us anything about Stephen's background. We don't know who his parents were or where he came from. We do not know anything about his profession or education or how long he had been a member of the church. We don't know whose preaching or witnessing lead to his conversion or who baptized him. Evidently that information was not important to the Scripture writers. What was important was the anointing that was on Stephen's life. What was important was the condition of his heart. What was important was his zeal for the Lord. What was important was the grace of the Lord that flowed through his life. What was important was the high regard that he was held in by the church, not because of the length of his membership or his hair or his robe but because of the way the power of the Holy Spirit worked through him and performed great signs and wonders among the people to the glory of God.

What sets us apart as believers is not our backgrounds. It is not how we dress or even how we talk. What makes us special is not how long we can claim membership in a particular church or our title. What makes us special is not the organizational or denominational label that is attached to our membership. What sets us apart as believers is our confession of faith that Jesus Christ is our Lord and Savior, which is the basis for the anointing of the Holy Spirit upon our lives. What sets us apart is the power of God that is able to work through us to bring forth miracles in our lives and in the lives of others. What sets us apart is our faith, and when we become cynical and negative we lose our distinctiveness. What sets us apart is our worship and praise, and when we can worship and praise God only when things go our way we lose our distinctiveness. What sets us apart is our boldness, and when we become timid and weak and fearful we lose our distinctiveness. What sets us apart is our newness, and when we become set in our ways we lose our distinctiveness.

What sets us apart is our generosity, and when we become cheap and stingy and grudging we lose our distinctiveness. What sets us apart is our joy, and when we become grumblers and gossips we lose our distinctiveness. What sets us apart is our peace, and when we become worriers and anxious we lose our distinctiveness. What sets us apart is our love and our compassion, and when we become self-centered and hard-hearted we lose our distinctiveness. What sets us apart is our prayer life, and when we start handling things and people our way we lose our distinctiveness.

What sets us apart is our transformed mind, and when we start thinking like everybody else and try to "keep up with the Joneses" we lose our distinctiveness. What sets us apart is the Word of God, and when we start being guided by others or by our own thinking we lose our distinctiveness. What sets us apart is our sweetness, and when we become rebellious we lose our distinctiveness. What sets us apart is our humility, and when we become self-righteous we lose our distinctiveness. What sets us apart is our strength, and when we become weak we lose our distinctiveness. What sets us apart is our faithfulness, and when we become quitters we lose our distinctiveness. What sets us apart is Jesus, and when we do not reflect Jesus we lose our distinctiveness.

And when we lose our distinctiveness, then others can lock us into their categories and limit our horizons, and we have no extra power or anointing to grow beyond the systems and classifications where others have placed us. But when we keep our distinctiveness, then we can outgrow our classification as a woman or a black or an unwed mother or an addict or an ex-con or a divorcee. For if anyone is in Christ Jesus he or she is a new creation; old things are passed away, behold all things become new. Colossians 3:1-2 becomes our theme: "So if you have been raised with Christ, seek the things that are above, where Christ is, seated at the right hand of God. Set your minds on things that are above, not on things that are on earth..."

Stephen was selected to be a helper to the Apostles and to serve in the capacity of bread distributor. He did not have the classification of an apostle. Yet when we read of his work in the Scriptures we see him preaching and teaching. We read of him performing great signs and wonders. We read of his defense before the Sanhedrin Council. As a matter of fact, his speech of fifty-three verses is one of the longest recorded speeches in the New Testament. The sermon preached by Peter on the Day of Pentecost was only twenty-five verses. Paul's sermon on Mars Hill was only nine verses. Paul's defense before Felix was only twelve verses, and his defense before King Agrippa was only twenty-nine verses. Outside of the Gospels the longest speech recorded in the New Testament was given by Stephen, who was neither one of the original twelve disciples called by Jesus nor one who was selected to fulfill the apostolic office in the life of the church. Stephen, who was categorized as a helper and one who waited on tables and served food to the needy, gave it. When we read Acts 7 we see that the preaching of Stephen before the Sanhedrin was so powerful that they could not stand it. They became enraged. Not even the preaching of Peter before them upset them so much as the preaching of non-apostle Stephen. The Word of God tells us that they became so enraged that they took Stephen out and stoned him.

As they were stoning Stephen he looked up into heaven and saw Jesus standing at the right hand of God. Usually when we read of Jesus at the right hand of God in the Scriptures he is seated. As a matter of fact, this is the only place where we read of Jesus standing at the right hand of God. We stand as a sign of respect. Jesus is standing in this passage as a sign of respect for one of his servants. He is standing to welcome one of his servants home. He is standing to get a better view of his child. But who is the servant that Jesus stands for? Is it John the beloved disciple? Is it Peter, the Rock? Is it Matthew, Mark, or Luke, writers of the Gospels? Is it his mother, Mary, or faithful Mary Magdalene? Was it his good friends and hosts—Mary, Martha, and Lazarus? Was it the great seer and revelator John of Patmos? We do not know how Jesus welcomed them or what sign of respect he gave to them, but the Scriptures tell us that he stood up for the non-apostle Stephen, who did not have a title but who was categorized as a helper and a distributor of bread.

As Stephen died, he prayed for his enemies saying, "Lord, do not hold this sin against him." His prayer sounds like the prayer Jesus prayed on Calvary, "Father, forgive them, for they do not know what they are doing." We do not know what prayers came from the lips of others who were martyred for their faith. I like to believe that many of them prayed the same prayer. But the Scriptures clearly record the words of Stephen. The only person recorded in Scripture whose dying words reflect those of Jesus when he was on the cross was non-titled, table-serving Stephen. He became the first martyr recorded in Scripture for the faith.

Evidently, no matter how Stephen was categorized in the life of the church, the anointing was so powerful upon him—the Spirit and power of God had so enriched his life—that he outgrew his category. He became as powerful in his witness and his work, and even in his death, as any of the apostles. Stephen outgrew his categories. He outgrew his title. Some of us live for our title. Some of us don't ever grow beyond the category others have put us in. Some believers are afraid to venture forth with a new suggestion or to come forth with our talents or our abilities because of the category we are in as a new member, or as a minority or as an ex-this or ex-that, or because we made a mistake or we have a certain background. And we know that others have pigeonholed us and cast us into a certain mold. And we dare not get out of our place and category. But we need to remember that God has not given us a spirit of timidity or fear. God has given us power and love and a sound mind. We need to remember that the anointing of God can so flow through us, and the power of God can so fill us, and the Spirit of God can so gift us, and the blood of Jesus can so cleanse us, and the gospel can so transform us, and the grace of God can so bless us that we can outgrow our categories.

Categories do not determine who we are, what we can do, or how far we can go. Our character, our vision, our faithfulness and perseverance, the Word of God, the Spirit of God, our self-image shaped by the second birth, the Holy Spirit, our growth in the grace and knowledge of our Lord and Savior Jesus Christ to whom all glory and honor are due—these are the factors that determine who we are and how far we can go. We can outgrow our categories if we think the right thoughts. That's what Paul was talking about when he said, "Finally, beloved, whatever is true, whatever is honorable, whatever is just, whatever is pure, whatever is pleasing, whatever is commendable, if there is any excellence and if there is anything worthy of praise, think about these things" (Philippians 4:8).

To be in Christ Jesus is not simply to outgrow our categories. It is to be unclassified. You can reach low to lift the fallen. You can stand in the middle of stress without breaking, and you can reach up to heaven in prayer. Jesus always defied classification. When he was born, angels from the highest heavens sang to low-class shepherds while middle-class wise men came from the East seeking him. During his lifetime those who believed in him included middle-class homeowners like Martha and Mary of Bethany, rich yet reformed tax collectors like Zacchaeus, and lower-class beggars like blind Bartimaeus. When Jesus died, the highest heaven shook the earth, a low-class thief was granted access to Paradise, and middle-class Nicodemus interceded for the body. How do we classify Jesus? He defies all of our categories and categorizations.

To the architect he is the chief cornerstone.
To the artist he is the one altogether lovely.
To the astronomer he is the Bright and Morning Star.
To the baker he is Living Bread.
To the bereaved he is the Resurrection and the Life.
To the biologist he is life.
To the botanist he is the Lily of the Valley.
To the businessman he is a good investment.
To the carpenter he is the door.
To the confused he is a mind regulator.
To the computer analyst he is the perfect program.
To the construction worker he is a good foundation.
To the convict he is a commuted sentence.
To the divorcee he is the perfect mate.
To the doctor he is the Great Physician.
To the electrician he is the light of the world.
To the engineer he is the Wheel in the Middle of the Wheel.
To the farmer he is the sower.

To the gambler he is a sure thing.
To the gardener he is the Rose of Sharon.
To the historian he is the Alpha and Omega.
To the homeless he is a shelter from the stormy blast.
To the humanist he is love unsurpassed.
To the judge he is true truth.
To the laborer he is a fair employer.
To the lawyer he is a new commandment.
To the lonely he is a friend who sticks closer than a brother.
To the mathematician he is the way.
To the militant he is a battle-axe.
To the old he is life eternal.
To the orphan he is the Everlasting Father.
To the philosopher he is the greatest of all paradoxes.
To the preacher he is prophet and priest.
To the romantic he is the fairest of ten thousand.
To the royalty he is Lord of Lords.
To the ruler he is the King of Kings.
To the sinner he is Savior.
To the statesman he is the Prince of Peace.
To the teacher he is the Great Rabbi.
To the weak he is a burden bearer.
To the widowed he is a constant companion.
To the young he is the Wonderful Counselor.

Growing Beyond Our Hesitations (or Reservations)

TEXT: ACTS 9:10-18

WHEN THE WORD of the Lord came to the believer Ananias in a vision and told him to go to a certain house and find Saul of Tarsus, Ananias had his reservations. Those reservations or that hesitation was not without merit. Saul's reputation as an enemy of the faith had preceded his arrival in Damascus. His attack upon the church in Jerusalem was well known, and his intentions to do the same thing in Damascus were also known. Thus when the instructions came to minister to Saul, Ananias understandably hesitated. The Lord explained to Ananias that he had work for Saul to do and that in the process of doing it Saul himself would experience the same kind of suffering he had tried to impose upon others. Ananias obeyed the Word of the Lord. He went to Saul and said to him, "Brother Saul, the Lord Jesus, who appeared to you on your way here, has sent me so that you may regain your sight and be filled with the Holy Spirit." The Word of God tells us that "immediately something like scales fell from his eyes, and his sight was restored. Then got up and was baptized, and after taking some food, he regained his strength."

In Ananias's obedience to the word of instruction that he received in the vision, he demonstrates a truth about the faith that we sometimes forget. Faith sometimes means being obedient in spite of our hesitations and reservations. Faith means following with reservations. This definition probably sounds a bit strange to a number of us because many of us tend to think that faith means swallowing everything "hook, line, and sinker." For many of us faith means being certain about what we believe. After all, the great definition of faith found in Hebrews 11:1 says that faith is "the assurance of things hoped for, the conviction of things not seen." For many of us faith means believing without doubting. For many of us faith means having everything settled and worked out in advance so that when we act, we do so from a position of strength, never wavering and not looking back.

However, I would submit to you that there are times when our faith will not be free from doubt, when we will have as many questions as we will have convictions. There will be times when we will not be so sure about how things are going to turn out. There will be times when, like Ananias, we will have good reason for doubting the Word of God. There will be times when, like Ananias, the Word of God will go against logic and common sense. There will be times when the Word of God will not compute with our own experiences with people or with some of our own experiences in life. Ananias's knowledge of Saul was that he was a vicious enemy of the faith. Thus if Saul was blind he was getting just what he deserved. The blindness of Saul was probably looked upon as a confirmation of Ananias's faith that Saul was on the wrong side and that he was being punished for what he did to the church in Jerusalem. The blindness of Saul was probably viewed by the early church as punishment and just desserts for all of the trouble Saul had caused. The blindness of Saul was probably viewed by Ananias and the early church as an answer to prayer and as the nullification of an enemy. The blindness of Saul was probably looked upon by Ananias and some of the members of the early church as a solution to a troublesome problem.

If you and I had been believers of the early church in Jerusalem and Saul had been responsible for disrupting our family life or causing us to lose our jobs or putting us or someone we loved in jail because we believed in Jesus, and we heard that he had been blinded and stopped on his way to do the same thing to a group of believers somewhere else, I can guess how most of us would have reacted and what most of us would have said when we heard that Saul was blind. We would have said: "Good! Praise God! He got just what he deserved. That just goes to show you that God really will fight our battles if you must keep still. Saul blind? I tell you God is good all the time." And can you imagine how we would have felt if we then received instructions from the Lord in the midst of our celebration, in the midst of our thanksgiving and praise, in the midst of our dance, that said, "Go heal him." We would have said: "Heal Saul? You must be kidding. After all the hell he raised, after all the pain he has caused to me personally, after what he did to my good friends or my loved ones back in Jerusalem, you want me to go heal him? God, surely you jest."

In the eyes of the believers like Ananias, Saul must have appeared to be the devil himself incarnate in human flesh. Yet when Ananias received the Word to go to Saul to lay his hands upon him and heal him, in spite of whatever hesitation he had, he obeyed. That for me is the essence of faith. Someone who has faith is not sure and confident all the time. Someone with faith has doubts and questions, does not have everything worked out and settled mentally or emotionally or spiritually, and is not always joyful and does not always follow God with a glad mind or willing spirit. Sometimes we will have our doubts and hesitations. Sometimes we will not feel like doing what the Word of God tells us to do. Sometimes we will not be sure about how things are going to turn out, yet still we are obedient and still we follow the Word of God. We follow the vision. We follow our hearts even when our minds or logic or our education or even our experience tell us to go the other way or to do just the opposite.

When we read the Scriptures we will discover that many of those who followed the Lord or followed what they perceived to be God's will for their lives had hesitations and reservations. Look at Peter and John and some of their companions after a hard, long night of unsuccessful fishing. They are frustrated, tired, disgusted, and perhaps a little discouraged. No matter what the endeavor is—whether it is fishing or a relationship or being faithful or praying or practicing for some event—it is always rough to put a lot of hard work into something and have nothing to show for it. After fishing all night long they have caught nothing. They have pulled their boat onto shore and are looking forward to some much-needed rest when Jesus tells them to launch out into the deep water and let down their nets for a catch. Peter, with his experience of last night's unsuccessful fishing trip fresh on his mind, justifiably expresses his hesitation and says, "Master, we have worked all night long but have caught nothing. Yet if you say so, I will let down the nets" (Luke 5:5).

Everyone the disciples talked to said that if Jesus returned to Jerusalem for the feast of the Passover, he would be killed. The hostility had reached a point at which Jesus' enemies were determined he would not leave Jerusalem alive. Yet Jesus steadfastly sets his face to go to Jerusalem, and there was nothing anyone could do or say to change his mind. Why would Jesus purposely put his own head in the mouth of a hungry lion? When there were other places that were open to his ministry and witness where he had enjoyed success, why would he go into territory that he knew was hostile and unreceptive? The disciples had their questions and grave reservations about Jesus going to Jerusalem, yet they followed him there nevertheless.

On the night before he died, even Jesus expressed some hesitation and reservation about Calvary. He was not afraid of the pain or the suffering. He was not afraid of the priest or the soldiers. He was not afraid of the devil or even of death. What got next to him was the realization that, in order to redeem us and save us from the hold of sin and the judgment of death, he as a sinless and righteous person would have to become the very embodiment and representative of the sin he had spent his whole life fighting against and living against. He realized that to redeem us, though he was without sin, he would have to become a sin offering. And he expressed reservations about becoming a representative of what he despised in order to save those whom he loved. Hear his prayer of reservations and hesitation: "O my Father, if it is possible let this bitter cup pass from me; nevertheless not what I will, but what you will."

The disciples, Ananias, and even our Lord had their reservations at times about doing what was required of them. Yet they were obedient to the Word that they received from heaven; they followed what they perceived to be God's will nevertheless; they followed as they were led. Growing is not always easy. Following God's vision for our lives will not always be easy. Doing the will of God and reaching the next level of our faith journey will not always be easy. For at times we will be told to do things that don't seem to make sense, that go against our logic or even our own experience. Sometimes we will have hesitations, reservations, and questions. However, that is what faith is all about: following God's Word, following God's will, following God's vision for our lives even when we have reservations. Faith is not the absence of questions; faith is being obedient even when we have questions. Faith is not the absence of doubt; faith means being obedient even when we have doubts. Faith is not the absence of reservations or hesitations; faith is being obedient even when we have reservations and hesitations. For if we waited until all of our doubts and questions were settled and answered, we would never act. Sometimes it is only as we act that God's will becomes clear, that the promises of God's Word are kept, that God's vision begins to unfold.

Someone may be saying to himself or herself, "I really would like to grow beyond my hesitation and reservation, but I do not know how." Ananias, the disciples, and Jesus all had their reservations, but they were obedient to the Word and the vision they received because they trusted the Word of God. How much do you trust the Word of God? Not the word of the preacher, but the Word of God. If you don't believe me, believe the Word that I represent. If you do not trust me, then trust the Word that I represent. Not the word of other people, but the Word of God. Not the word of the Constitution or the U.S. government, but the Word of God. Not the latest financial report or scientific document, but the Word of God. I refer to the Word of God that made the heavens and the earth. I refer to the Word of God that wakes the sun up every morning and tells the stars to twinkle at night. I refer to the Word of God that says to the ocean's swelling tides when their might would break down dams and sweep over the land, "This far and no farther." I refer to the Word of God that has never broken a promise or proven to be unreliable since it was first uttered. How much do you trust the Word of God? Faith says, "I may not understand the Word of God, but I trust the Word of God." Faith says, "I may not agree or even like the Word of God sometimes, but I trust the Word of God." Faith says, "I have my hesitations and my doubts, but I still trust the Word of God." Faith says, "Sometimes my own experience in life and my own experience with people do not jibe or connect with the Word of God, but I still trust the Word of God. Therefore I follow it; I submit to it; I am obedient to it in spite of my reservation and hesitations."

I know that some of us have our own hesitations about tithing. Our own experience dictates—our logic tells us—that when we have bills to pay and insufficient money to meet obligations, we do not give ten percent of our income off of the top to God through his church. Our own logic says that when we look at ten percent of what God has blessed us to make, that is too much money to give to the church. But hear the Word of God: "Bring the full tithe into the storehouse..." (Malachi 3:10). How much do you trust the Word of God?

I know that some of us are hesitant about joining the church or changing churches. I know that some of us have had unpleasant and disappointing experiences with ministers and some church people. I know that some are afraid that if we join the church we will be disappointed again, that the preacher will be moved or that he or she will leave again. I know that some of us don't understand everything we would like to understand about the church we are thinking about joining. I know that some of us are concerned about what our family or our friends will think if we leave the church where we were born or raised or the church where we have belonged because it no longer meets our growing needs. I know that some of us feel that our own family or friends will be hurt if we leave them where they are. Their hurt is real and those concerns are real, and I do not take them lightly. But how much do you trust the Word of God? If the Word of God and the Spirit of God are pulling you to join a new church home, trust the Word of God and the Spirit of God. God knows how to take care of those you are concerned about. God says to us, "I know that you have reservations and I know that you have concerns, but trust me. Follow the Word that I have placed in your heart and in your spirit. I will take care of you, but to see how I will do it, you must follow, you must obey, you must surrender even with your reservations and hesitations."

God says, "I know that the decision about that new job or that promotion or that new relationship or that new opportunity is a difficult one to make. But you also know my Word. If what you are involved in is against my Word or if that new opportunity is against my Word, then, no matter how appealing it is, trust my Word. I will give you what you seek; I will give you your heart's desire without your compromising your principles or without your compromising my Word. And if what you seek is consistent with the Word of God, then seek my will and wait for me to speak. And when you receive my Word to you, then obey, even if you have hesitations and doubt." How much do you trust the Word of God?

God says to us, "I know that the church is going in some new directions that are different from what you have been accustomed to. I know that you have hesitations and reservations about some of this new music and new styles of worship and praise. I know that you have questions and reservations about all of this language about the Holy Spirit. I know that some of the things you see happening in churches today go against your tradition or your teaching or your understanding about what is proper decorum in church, in worship, in music, and even in preaching. I know that for you church isn't like it used to be and you are uncomfortable about seeing so many of the old familiar landmarks changed and removed. However, is what you see happening inconsistent with my Word? That is the standard that you are to use. Does not my Word say to make a joyful noise unto the Lord? Does not my Word say to come into my presence with singing and into my courts with praise? What makes you think that the only singing that is acceptable to me is an anthem or a hymn or gospel? Does not my Word say to tithe? Does not my Word say that in the last days I will pour out my Spirit upon all flesh and that your sons and daughters will prophesy?" If what is happening in the church is consistent with God's Word, then how much do you trust the Word of God when it comes to instructing us about the worship and character of the church's life? If we trust the Word of God, then we obey the Word of God even if we have questions and some hesitations.

In spite of his hesitation and reservations, Ananias obeyed the Word of God. By the way, who was Ananias? Frankly we do not know anything about him other than what appears in this chapter. After he ministers to Saul we do not hear from him again. If he had not grown beyond his reservations when the Word of the Lord came to him, if he had objected to receiving Saul into the church, if he had disobeyed or fought the Word of the Lord that came to him, I doubt if his name would have made it into the record. However, because he was willing to grow beyond whatever hesitation he may have had, his name is in the book and his deed is in the record. By the way, who were the disciples? Who were Peter, James, John, and the others? They were just ordinary, dime-a-dozen Galilean Jews. If they had not been associated with Jesus, if they had not been obedient to the Word of the Lord when it came to them, I doubt if we would know anything about them. But because they were willing to grow beyond whatever vision of life they may have had for themselves and accept Christ's call and Word to them, their names are in the book and their deeds are in the record.

Who was Jesus Christ? He was a righteous man, a good teacher, a powerful preacher, and a mighty worker of miracles. However, there have been a number of good teachers, powerful preachers, righteous persons, and miracle workers, none of whom are celebrated as Savior of the world and Lord of history. If Jesus had not moved beyond his reservations, voiced in his agony in Gethsemane—if he had not said yes when the Word from his Father was for him to go to Calvary—I doubt if we would be worshipping him as King of Kings and Lord of Lords. If he had not grown beyond his reservations in Gethsemane, there would have been no Calvary, and without Calvary there would have been no redemption of sin and no victory over the grave to celebrate. Without a victory over the grave, there would have been no opportunity for Jesus to ascend to heaven and prepare a place for us. Without the redemption of sin and victory over the grave, there would have been no promise and no need for a baptism of the Holy Spirit. Without the redemption of sin and the victory over the grave, there would be no need to promise that he would come again and take us unto himself to be forever with the Lord. However, because Jesus did move beyond his hesitation, we have a song that not even the angels can sing: "Redeemed, redeemed, we've been redeemed." Because he did move beyond his reservations we, who were once far off, have been brought near. We who were lost have been found, and we who were grave-destined and hell-bound have become "a chosen race, a royal priesthood, a holy nation, God's own people, in order that [we] may proclaim the mighty acts of him who called [us] out of darkness into his marvelous light" (1 Peter 2:9).

We have become who we are with the faith, the salvation, and the access to the throne of God because Jesus moved beyond his hesitation in Gethsemane and said yes to his Father's will and Word. The Lord may have brought some of us a long ways, for which we praise God. However, what may really cause us to have our finest hour is our willingness to grow beyond whatever hesitations we may have now and move to the next level to which God is calling us. One thing I am sure of is that we won't get there without tithing. We won't get there outside of a church with a vision for growth. We won't get there by being disobedient to the Word of God. We won't get there unless we are open to a new move of the Spirit that may take us beyond our present comfort zones. We will never know what God has in store for us if we do not grow beyond our hesitations. Eyes have not seen nor have ears heard; neither has it been revealed in our hearts the good things God has in store for those who are obedient to his Word, who grow beyond their hesitations, who are willing to say, "Yes, Lord! Yes, Lord! Yes Lord!"

Growing Beyond a Narrow Vision

TEXT: ACTS 11:1-3 AND PHILIPPIANS 4:13

FOR ANYONE INTERESTED in growth, the Book of Acts is a good place to start. The very name "Acts" implies growth because growth is action. We do not grow by being still. Growth means that something is expanding or stretching or lengthening. Growth means action. In Acts 1 the church is growing in prayer; the Day of Pentecost was preceded by prayer and ushered in through prayer. No prayer, no growth! In Acts 2 we see the church growing in spiritual power, in numbers, and in love. After power fell on the church on the Day of Pentecost, three thousand souls joined the church as Peter proclaimed the truth of the gospel. The day of Pentecost changed the character of the church's life; the members showed such caring for each other that they held all things in common and distributed to all persons according to their needs. No spiritual power, no growth. No Holy Spirit, no growth. No Holy Spirit and no spiritual power, no love among church members. In other words, when the Holy Spirit is present, there is not only power, but there is also love among believers.

In Acts 3 in the healing of the man born lame, we see the church growing in the exercise of its spiritual gifts. We grow as we use whatever gifts the Holy Spirit bestows upon each of us. In the defense of Peter and John before the Sanhedrin Council in Acts 4, we see the church growing beyond fear of the opposition. Fear stifles growth. In Acts 5 in the incident involving Ananias and Sapphira, we see the church growing in its discipline, even of its very own. We cannot grow without discipline and without bringing in line that which is out of order. In Acts 6 we see the church growing as it deals with the stuff of inner turmoil that arose because the Greek-speaking widows felt they were being neglected in the daily distribution of bread. Stuff will hamper growth unless we deal with it. In Acts 7 we see the church growing as the Holy Spirit powerfully used Stephen even though he had a so-called lesser office. One's position or one's title has nothing to do with either one's anointing or one's effectiveness.

In Acts 8 we see the church grow as persecution broke out against it in Jerusalem and believers such as Philip were forced to proclaim the gospel elsewhere. One can grow even in difficult circumstances. The issue for growth is not hard times, but how we handle hard times when they come. Also in Acts 8 we see the church grow as the Samaritans receive the baptism of the Holy Spirit that breaks centuries of generational bondage. Growth means that we grow beyond some of our baggage from the past. We cannot grow taking all of the baggage that we have inherited or acquired along the way. In order to grow we are going to have to get rid of some things. In Acts 9 we see growth with the conversion of Saul, who had been an enemy of the church. Growth means being big enough to forgive those who have hurt us. No forgiveness, no growth. Perhaps some of us are not receiving all that the Lord has for us because of how we feel about certain people.

In Acts 10, with the conversion of Gentiles, the church makes another broad step in its spiritual and numeric growth. Lest we forget, the first believers were Jews who had accepted Jesus Christ as the Messiah, the Anointed of God. Consequently, even though they were believers in Jesus, many of them still practiced the tenets and held on to the beliefs of their Judaic faith. They were like so many of us who believe in Jesus but who still hold on to many of our former ways. Even though we are followers of Jesus, we still like to participate in questionable lifestyles, use language, and think thoughts that we should have grown beyond and left behind. Even though we are followers of Jesus, we are still trying to serve several masters.

When I went to the circus as a little boy, I noticed that the lion tamer, in addition to his whip, would always have a chair. It was a long time before I learned why a chair was an effective means for taming and controlling lions. When the lion tamer pointed the chair at the lion, the lion would always try to focus on all four legs at one time, and thus he became paralyzed. Perhaps that is why so many of us cannot grow as we should. We are trying to focus on too much at one time. Rather than trying to focus on God's vision of growth for our lives, we are trying to focus on our wills, what somebody else has, our security, our money, our careers, our pleasures, and our carnality. Rather than focusing on the Word of God, which tells us to seek first the kingdom of God and its righteousness with the promise that other things will be provided in abundance, we focus on the other things and become paralyzed in our growth.

Even when the members of the early church heard Jesus' command to carry the gospel to all nations, they were thinking about carrying that gospel to Jews in other nations or to those who were just like themselves. In the text that comes from Acts 11 the church and its individual members have another opportunity to grow beyond a narrow vision of God and of themselves. Narrowness stifles growth. We can grow only as broadly as we think. What is narrow thinking? When we look at the text we see narrow thinking in action. When news reached some of the members of the early church about the conversion of Gentiles, what was their reaction? One would expect that they would have been excited that the gospel had made such an inroad. However, because they were functioning within the narrow vision that the gospel was for Jews only, they became insulted and offended. They criticized Peter, asking him, "Why did you go to the uncircumcised men and eat with them?"

The members of the church who were critical of Peter's action in taking the gospel to the Gentiles were functioning with a narrow vision of themselves as the people of God. They failed to realize that being followers of Jesus meant getting rid of old prejudices, old feuds, and old divisions. They failed to realize that being followers of Christ Jesus meant building new relationships with those from whom they had felt distant in the past. Is this the reason some of us are not growing? We are not prepared to let go of some of our old prejudices, old misunderstandings, and old hostilities toward certain people. Some of us have to realize that a new creation and old conflicts don't mix. New blessings and old bitterness don't mix. New holiness and old hostilities don't mix. New heights and old hatreds don't mix. New worship and new work and new ways and old warfare don't mix. New faith and old feuds don't mix. New power and old prejudices don't mix. New spirituality and old spitefulness don't mix. New redemption and old racism don't mix. New salvation and old sexism don't mix. New deliverance and old division don't mix. New freedom and old fights don't mix. New giving and old greed do not mix. A new Savior and old stinginess do not mix. New growth and old grudges do not mix. A new anointing and old anger do not mix. A new testimony and old thinking do not mix.

The straight and narrow way does not mean that we have to be straight and narrow in our thinking. We "can't" be big and small at the same time. The tragedy with so many of us is that we have opted for smallness when God has so much more in store for us. We have opted for narrowness when God wants to broaden us to receive all that God has for us. Whenever we use the word "can't," that's smallness and that's narrowness. I personally believe that "can't" is one word that ought to be banished from a Christian's vocabulary. When the very God who created the heavens and the earth has personally pledged to answer our prayers and to provide for our needs, the word "can't" should not even be in our vocabulary. When we claim that we believe that "God so loved [us] that he gave his only Son, so that everyone who believes in him may not perish but may have eternal life" (John 3:16), the word "can't" should not even be in our vocabulary. When we have the Holy Spirit in our lives, when we have God living within us, when we have God's power living within us, the word "can't" ought not to even be in our vocabulary. When we have the promises of God's Word that have never been broken or revoked operational in our lives, the word "can't" ought not even be in our vocabulary.

When God's Word has promised that all things are ours, the word "can't" ought not to even be in our vocabulary. When God's Word has promised that no weapon formed against us shall prosper, the word "can't" ought not to even be in our vocabulary. God's Word has assured us that God, who did not spare his only son for us, will also give us all things with him. The word "can't" ought not even be in our vocabulary. When God's Word has assured us that God's desire for us is that we should be the head and not the tail, the word "can't" should not even be in our vocabulary. When God's Word has assured us that God's grace is sufficient for us and that God's strength is made perfect in our weakness, the word "can't" should not even be in our vocabulary. When God's Word has assured us that we are God's children now—and it does not yet appear what we shall be, but when Christ shall appear we shall be like him for we shall see him as he is—the word "can't" should not even be in our vocabulary. When God's Word has assured us that if we resist the devil, then the devil will flee from us, the word "can't" should not even be in our vocabulary.

When God's Word has assured us that one can chase a thousand and two put ten thousand to flight (Deuteronomy 32:30), the word "can't" should not even be in our vocabulary. When Jesus has told us that it is God's good pleasure to give to us the kingdom, the word "can't" should not even be in our vocabulary. When Jesus has told us that we have the keys to the kingdom and that whatever we bind on earth shall be bound in heaven and that whatever we loose on earth shall be loosed in heaven, the word "can't" should not even be in our vocabulary. When the Word of God has assured us that greater is the power that is within us than any power that is in the world, the word "can't" should not even be in our vocabulary. When God has promised never to leave us or forsake us, the word "can't" should not even be in our vocabulary.

If we want to unlock our potential and maximize our growth,

if we desire to achieve and receive all that God has in store for us, if we want to do ourselves a favor, the best thing that we can do is to make a vow and pledge never to use the word "can't" again. Forget about it. For you the word does not exist. Dig a hole, bury the word, cover the hole up, and then forget the place where you have buried it.

No matter how young we are, we can do all things through Christ who strengthens us. No matter how old we are, we can do all things through Christ who strengthens us. No matter how sick we are we can do all things through Christ who strengthens us. No matter what mistakes we have made in the past or what weaknesses we have, we can do all things through Christ who strengthens us. No matter how many times we have failed, we can still do all things through Christ who strengthens us. No matter who tells us what we cannot or dare not do, we can do all things through Christ who strengthens us. No matter how poor we are, we can still do all things through Christ who strengthens us. No matter what our background is or who our parents are, we can do all things through Christ who strengthens us. No matter who called us dumb or told us that we could not learn or that we could not be a success, we can do all things through Christ who strengthens us.

We can go back to school and graduate even at this point in our lives. We can have a successful relationship with the opposite sex. We can have the righteous desires of our hearts. We can tithe. We can make it. We can be delivered from that habit that has us bound. We can stop smoking. We can be free from caffeine addiction. We can be delivered from food and from lust and from lying and gossip. We can be delivered from pettiness, narrowness, and small-mindedness. We can be delivered from depression, negative thinking, whining, and complaining. We can be delivered from looking for the worst in people and always expecting the worst to happen. We can be delivered from our fears and insecurities and guilt.

The devil is a liar. People do not really know the potential that God has placed within us, and so their judgment is often wrong and is definitely not final. Our best is yet to come, no matter how old we are. *We can truly do all things through Christ who strengthens us.*

To grow beyond narrowness we have to grow beyond old feelings about others and begin to walk in the power and the victory that we have in Christ Jesus. Those who criticized Peter for taking the gospel to the Gentiles not only had a narrow vision of themselves; they also had a narrow vision of God, Jesus, and the gospel. They were acting as if Jesus was their own personal possession, that his death and spilled blood upon Calvary was only for their sins, that the resurrection was only for their victory over death, and that the promise of the second coming was only for their faithfulness. They were acting as if the gospel of salvation and deliverance was only for them. They were begrudging others for receiving what they had received as if they were going to lose something they had received if somebody else received it also. They were evidently not secure in who they were as the redeemed children of God.

Is that why some of us are so possessive and so protective of our turf and our positions? Is our problem that we come from such backgrounds of poverty of dearth and lack and insufficiency that one could not receive unless another was denied? Did someone take something from us that we thought was ours, and now we feel that we have to hold and hoard and protect what we feel belongs to us? Is that why we are so suspicious and sometimes unwelcoming to new people with gifts or talents or looks or youth or experience or ability or an opinion or a brain or class? Is that why some of us feel that we have to put new people through our own initiation process and investigation to see what they are made of, where they come from, and what they are about?

Who appointed or anointed us to be watchdogs and clearinghouses for those who come to the Lord and have a desire to immediately become involved in the church rather than waiting around for twenty years like some of us had to do until somebody died? Who are we to insist that others pass our standards of acceptance before they can hold an office or have an idea or voice an opinion or lead anything? Why are we so protective and possessive about our ministries, our songs, our seats, our jobs and responsibilities, our titles and positions? Why are we so worried about somebody taking our place or our power or what we believe belongs exclusively to us? Why do we use the word "my" in connection with what really belongs to the Lord? My program, my ministry, my ushers, my trustees, my stewards, my choir, my solo, my seat. What is it in our background that makes us so insecure and so possessive about what the Lord has allowed us to have or receive or achieve?

The good news that I bring to all of us today is that we can relax in the good news and the bounty of God. God has enough blessings, enough glory, enough power, enough titles, enough work, and enough positions, for every person who is ready to receive them. God has a vision of greatness beyond anything that we can imagine for all of our lives. God does not have the same vision for each of us, but God does have a vision for each of us that is greater than anything we can imagine for ourselves. What God does for somebody else and what God gives to somebody else has nothing to do with what God has for us and what God has given to us. Instead of functioning in a paradigm of dearth or insufficiency where one cannot have unless someone is denied, God functions in a system of abundance. God has so much to give that everybody can have more than enough. For the earth is the Lord's and the fullness thereof. The cattle upon a thousand hills belong to God. Buried within the bowels of the earth God has placed abundant supplies of gold and silver, rubies, and diamonds that are waiting to be discovered. God has put ideas into our brains that are just waiting for us to speak them into being and give them birth. God has put potential into our lives that is waiting to be released. God has given us dreams and visions that are waiting for us to act upon them.

However, what God shows us is sometimes so big—for God does not deal in small visions—that when we see them, we say "I can't." And so they never come forth. Yet when somebody else pursues the visions God has given them and attains success, we become jealous and say, "God, why didn't you do that for me?" God says to us, "I wanted to, but you didn't let me. I wanted to, but you let the devil tell you what you could not do, or you allowed the devil to distract you. I wanted to, but you listened to the opinions of others who did not see what I showed you. I wanted to, but you were not willing to pay the price of hard work and discipline and sacrifice to get where I wanted to take you. I wanted to, but you would not tithe and I could not open the windows of heaven to you and pour down upon you the overflowing blessing. I wanted to, but you were too afraid of losing the little that you had or you were too comfortable with the half cup when I had an overflowing cup available for you. I wanted to, but you were so busy talking about what you could not do that you forgot that with me you could do all things. You forgot that if you follow the vision that I have for you, you are not in the battle for success and victory by yourself. I am with you, and I will make ways out of no ways and supply what you need. For when you follow me and opposition mounts and obstacles appear, the battle is not yours but mine."

Our problem in not having more is not what others receive, for God has plenty more of what has been given to them. Our problem is our narrow vision. I don't need to envy you because of your car when God has plenty of cars. I don't need to envy you for your success when God has plenty of success left. I don't need to envy you because of your relationships. God has plenty of available and eligible men and women left. What makes you think that there is only one fish in the sea? Perhaps you need to stop using that cane pole in the pond and start trolling in the ocean. Perhaps part of our problem is that our vision is so narrow—and we have chosen to keep our world small and comfortable—that God can bless us only so much because of where we have chosen to remain.

Our problem is not other people or opposition or obstacles. Our God is able to close the mouths of hungry and mean lions. Our God is able to level mountains, raise up valleys, straighten out the crooked, and make smooth that which is rough. The reason a number of us do not have more is us; our vision is too narrow.

We need to ask God to help us get ourselves out of the way so that we can see God's abundance. When we realize how much

God has and how much God has for us, then we will realize that we don't have to undercut anybody or be jealous of anybody or talk down anybody's success. So what if the Gentiles receive the gospel? So what if those with whom I have difficulty are blessed? So what if our enemies have success? God still has salvation for us. God still has deliverance for us. God still has eternal life for us. God still has abundance for us. God still has demon-defying and demon-breaking power for us. God still has miracles for us. God still has the desires of our hearts for us. God still has answers to prayers for us. God still has eternal life for us.

Grow Until It Doesn't Matter

TEXT: MATTHEW 21:1-11

APPROXIMATELY THREE YEARS prior to the first Palm Sunday celebration, when Jesus was just beginning his itinerant ministry, he had called Philip, a fellow resident from the northern region of Galilee, to be his disciple. Immediately after his call, Philip found his good friend Nathaniel and greeted him with the words, "We have found him about whom Moses in the law and also the prophets wrote, Jesus son of Joseph from Nazareth" (John 1:45-46, paraphrased). Nathaniel, who was sitting under a fig tree, looked up at his good friend and replied, "Did you say Jesus from Nazareth? Can anything good come out of Nazareth?"

Although Nathaniel was a northern Jew himself, in his sarcastic comment about Nazareth, which was also located in the north, Nathaniel reflected the disdain that many southern Jews had about their northern cousins. Many of the Jews in the southern region of Palestine—known as Judea, in which Jerusalem was located—looked upon their northern cousins with an air of superiority and at times contempt. A number of the southern Jews considered themselves to be the pure breeds of their ancestry while they looked upon their cousins from the north as half-breeds, or at least as people who were most susceptible to corruption from outside influences and other cultures. The Jews in the south considered themselves to be the purists who had kept the faith of their ancestors intact and without taint or blemish.

Cities such as Nazareth in the northern region of Palestine, known as Galilee, were looked upon as unsophisticated hick towns with no semblance of culture or class.

When one considers how Nazareth and the persons who came from it were viewed, the reaction of Jerusalem to Jesus on that first Palm Sunday was amazing indeed. According to the text, when Jesus approached Jerusalem during the Passover festivities, a large and enthusiastic crowd accompanied him. They were so excited that as he sat on the colt that had been brought for him people cut branches from the trees and spread them on the road. And they shouted, "Hosanna to the Son of David! Blessed is the one who comes in the name of the Lord! Hosanna in the highest heaven!" According to the text, when Jesus entered Jerusalem, the whole city was in turmoil. People saw the caravan and the excitement of the crowds and the man in the center of the commotion riding a donkey. And those who didn't know him asked the question, "Who is this?"

Let me just pause here to say that this question of who Jesus really is is the most important question any of us will ever have to answer. For the answer we give to that question will determine how we live now, what we live by, whom we live for, and where we will live when this life is over. Who is Jesus to you? Is he somebody who we have heard or read about, but have never really met? If that is what he is, then for you he is a rumor instead of a redeemer. Who is Jesus to you? Is he a historic figure we have read about in books? If that is what he is, then for you he is in the past and not in the present when we need him. Who is Jesus to you? Is he just another religious teacher or guru among others? If that is what he is, then all he can ever be is a dispenser of lessons and not a deliverer of life. Who is Jesus to you? Is he someone we have judged based upon the conduct of his followers? If that is what he is, then all he can ever be to you is secondhand and not a Savior.

Who is Jesus to you? Is he primarily a political activist? If that is all that he is to you, then you might know him as a revolutionary but not as a reconciler. Who is Jesus to you? Is he somebody who is meek and gentle? If that is all that he is, then you will never know him as a mighty God. Who is Jesus to you? Is he a healer of sickness? If that is all that he is to you, then you will never know him as a sanctifier from sin. Who is Jesus to you? Is he just a social worker who solves all of our social problems? If that is what he is, then you will never know what he can do for your soul. Who is Jesus to you? Is he a guarantor of material prosperity? If that is what he is, then you will never know the power he gives when you have nothing left but faith in him. Who is Jesus to you? Is he a prophet as described in today's text? If that is all he is, then you will never know him as the fulfillment of all that he proclaims. Prophets point to the way, but Jesus proclaims, "I am the Way." Prophets point to the truth, but Jesus says, "I am Truth." Prophets talk about life, but Jesus proclaims, "I am Life."

Who is Jesus to you? There are those who say that all religions teach the same things. There are parallels in all religions to be sure. But not all religions teach the same things, particularly about Jesus, who is the author and perfecter of our faith. For we Christians, Jesus is more than a religious teacher. Jesus is God incarnate—living, breathing, suffering, striving with the devil, victorious in human flesh. He is the highest expression of God's love for us, for God could not show any greater love than to become human flesh in order to show us our possibilities. Jesus is our eternal reminder that we matter to God. Our tears and our trials, our problems and our pain, our potential and our prayers, our futures and our families—all matter to God. Jesus is the Savior from sin. Whatever wrong we have done and whatever wrong we will ever do has already been forgiven when we, with repentant hearts, lift up the name of Jesus. He is Lord of our lives. He loves us so much that he is able to redeem us from sin and transform us into new and better persons. He is Lord of our lives. We live for him and we love him with all that we have and all that we are.

Not only is he Lord, but he is living. He walks with us. He talks with us. He tells us that we are his own. And when we stumble and fall he picks us up, cleans us off, and gives us another chance. But not only is Jesus the living Lord of our personal lives, he is Lord of history. In that he is raised from the dead, ultimate power in heaven and in earth is entrusted into his hands. And one day he is coming back again as judge of the world and to reward those who love and serve him. He is King of Kings and he is Lord of Lords and he reigns forever.

Who is Jesus to you? I have told you what he means to some of us. The good news I bring is that he will be the same thing to you if you let him. He will be a friend who sticks closer than any brother or sister. He is a father who never fails, a mother who is always near, and a loved one who never dies. He is a true and faithful companion. When you are torn down, he will restore you. When your heart is broken, he will mend it. When your mind is confused, he will be your guide. When you are lonely, he will be your forever lover. When you make a mistake, he will give you another chance. When your path is blocked, he will be your way-maker.

When some of those observed the tumult that surrounded Jesus on that first Palm Sunday they asked, "Who is this?" I wish I had time to walk through the Scriptures and tell who Jesus is. He is Daniel's stone hewn out of the mountain. He is Jeremiah's mighty battle-axe. He is Ezekiel's wheel in the middle of a wheel. He is one whom Isaiah described as "Wonderful Counselor, Mighty God, Everlasting Father, [and] Prince of Peace" (Isaiah 9:6). He is Solomon's Lily of the Valley and Rose of Sharon. He is Zechariah's branch. He is the Bright and Morning Star referred to in Numbers 24:17. He is David's chief cornerstone that the builders rejected. He is Jacob's lion of the tribe of Judah. He is John the Baptist's Lamb of God who takes away the sins of the world. He is the Samaritan woman's Living Water. He is Mary's, Martha's, and Lazarus's Resurrection and the Life. He is John the Revelator's Alpha and Omega, the beginning and the end, the first and the last.

Who is this?" asked some of those in crowd concerning Jesus on that first Palm Sunday. They received the answer, "This is the prophet Jesus from Nazareth in Galilee." Note the answer: "This is the prophet Jesus *from Nazareth in Galilee.*" They did not say that this is Jesus the prophet from one of the great rabbinical schools located in and around Jerusalem. They did not say that this is Jesus the prophet from lower or upper Jerusalem. They did not say that this is Jesus from the desert region south of Jerusalem. They said, "This is the prophet Jesus *from Nazareth in Galilee,*" of all places! The Scriptures do not record any negative reaction to his being from Galilee. There is no indication that the parade suddenly stopped and the cheering crowd suddenly started booing or that the festive celebration suddenly turned into a riot when it was announced that Jesus was from Nazareth in Galilee. I doubt that the prejudice and the arrogance that southern Jews had toward those from the north had suddenly disappeared. It was still there, but evidently Jesus had transcended it at that moment. Where he came from, the circumstances of his birth, who his parents were—all were evidently of no consequence at that moment during those first Palm Sunday festivities.

Evidently things had changed over the three-year period that elapsed since Nathaniel first uttered his sarcastic comment, "Can anything good come out of Nazareth?" (John 1:46). Jesus' reputation as God's prophet, as God's anointed, spirit filled, demon breaking, miracle working, death defying, compassionate chosen vessel was such that where he came from was of no importance to those who received him on that first Palm Sunday. If Mary, Martha, and Lazarus or those who had witnessed the raising of Lazarus from the dead had been present on that day the fact that Jesus came from Nazareth would not have mattered at all. They would have continued to praise him. If anyone who had been present when Jesus fed the five thousand with two fish and five barley loaves had been in the crowd on that first Palm Sunday, the fact that Jesus had come from Nazareth would not have mattered to them at all. They would have continued to praise him. If any one of those rejected lepers whom Jesus cleansed had been in the crowd that day, the fact that he came from Nazareth would not have mattered to them at all. They would have continued to praise him. If the man who had laid beside the pool of Bethesda had been in the crowd that day, the fact that Jesus had come from Nazareth would not have mattered to him at all. He would have waved his hands in praise. If any of those whose lives had been tormented and possessed by demons had been in the crowd that day, the fact that Jesus came from Nazareth would not have mattered to them at all. They would have continued to sing, "I once was lost, but now I'm found." And those who had been blind and had been healed would not have cared that he came from Nazareth. They would have had to join in and sing, "I was blind, but now I see."

At the moment of the Palm Sunday celebration, Jesus had grown so much in who he was as God's servant, the fact that he was raised in Nazareth, the fact that he was a carpenter's son, the fact that his mother became pregnant with him through the Holy Spirit before her union with Joseph was consummated—none of it mattered. Although he was from Nazareth, Jesus had so outgrown Nazareth—put it so far in his past—that his being from Nazareth did not matter to those whose lives he touched. The fact that he was from Nazareth did not affect the praise and thanksgiving and the love of those whose lives he had turned around and saved. Nazareth did not affect his power over demons or the anointing that was upon his life or the way he was able to bless people or the miracles he was able to perform. Nazareth did not affect the righteousness of his life or the truth that came from his lips or his life. Nazareth did not affect his ability to heal the sick, raise the dead, love children, or show compassion to those who were suffering.

We can grow so much as the children of God, as the redeemed of God, that some things people throw up in our faces won't matter anymore. We can grow so much as the redeemed children of God that where we came from or our past won't matter anymore. No matter what our past is, who our parents were or were not, or what neighborhood we came from, we can put so much distance between where we started and what we can become in Christ that what we used to be and what we once did won't matter any more.

You may have been born in poverty, but you don't have to stay in poverty. You may have been born in the mud, but you don't have to stay in the mud. You may have been born in the basement, but you don't have to stay in the basement. You may have been born in sin, but you don't have to stay in sin. With Jesus in your life you can rise so high that your beginnings in the basement or in the mud or in poverty won't matter. All people will see is what you have become. And when someone who knows about your past tries to pull you down, others will look at what you have become and say, "I don't know what they used to be, but I know what they are now. They are saved now. They are educated now. They have the anointing of God, the power of God, and the Word of God all through their life now. They have character and class now. They have prosperity now. They are good companions and mates now. So what if they came from Nazareth? Look at what they have become now. Look at where they are now. Look at what they have made of their lives now. Look at where the Lord has brought them. Hosanna in the highest heaven... Blessed is the one who comes in the name of the Lord!"

You can outgrow your guilt. You can outgrow your fears. You can outgrow that addiction. You can outgrow those mistakes. You can outgrow that sexual misconduct. You can outgrow the unwanted pregnancy. You can outgrow your co-dependency. You can outgrow that disastrous relationship. You can outgrow that divorce. You can outgrow that abuse. You can outgrow that temper. You can outgrow that cigarette. You can outgrow that attachment to money. You can outgrow that insecurity. You can outgrow that failure. You can outgrow that low self-esteem. You can outgrow that dysfunctional family. You can outgrow those bad choices. You can outgrow those friends or peer group who are trying to keep you where *they* are.

God can do such a mighty work in and with your life that the only thing that will matter is what you have become and how much you have grown. No matter where you have come from or your personal history, God's anointing can flow through you mightily. Love can grow from your life like a towering oak tree. Virtue can burst from your life like the dawn after a long midnight. Power can spread from your life like fire. Excellence can glow in your life like the stars. Peace can rest upon your life like the dew. The Word of God can fill your life like water fills the ocean floor. Salvation can kiss your life and hold you close like a lover. And those lives you have touched will rise up and call you blessed.

"When he entered Jerusalem, the whole city was in turmoil, asking, 'Who is this?' The crowds were saying, 'This is the prophet Jesus from Nazareth in Galilee.'" Perhaps we could understand this reception to Jesus occurring in Jericho where he healed blind Bartimaeus, but not Jerusalem. We could see it happening in Bethlehem, where he was born, but not Jerusalem. We could see it happening in Cana, where he performed his first miracle, but not Jerusalem. We could see it happening in Bethany, where he raised Lazarus, but not Jerusalem. After all, Jerusalem was the seat and center of conservative Orthodox Judaism, where that is not supposed to happen. It would be the last place one would expect to see a prophet from Nazareth honored. When God begins to move in your life it's amazing what God will do. God will not only allow you to outgrow your past to the point that it can't hurt or hinder what God will do in your life, but God will cause you to blossom in places and before people where it is not supposed to happen. You can never tell not only how high you can grow with God, but how far your reach can spread with God. God will elevate you in the most unlikely places. That's what David was talking about when he testified about God's goodness in his life: "You prepare a table before me in the presence of my enemies" (Psalm 23:5).

"When he entered Jerusalem, the whole city was in turmoil, asking, 'Who is this?' The crowds were saying, 'This is the prophet Jesus form Nazareth in Galilee.'" That's a long way from Nathaniel's statement three years earlier: "Can anything good come out of Nazareth?" It took three years for Jesus to outgrow Nazareth to the point that Nazareth didn't matter, but it didn't take forever. It takes time for us to outgrow the stigma of Nazareth, but it does not take forever. When you give your life to the Lord, one of the things you will discover is how quickly God can turn your life around. It will take time, but it will not take forever. It will take time for enemies to become footstools, but it will not take forever. It will take time for us to live down some of our mistakes. It will take time for us to become new persons in Christ Jesus, but it will not take forever. It will take time to receive the full blessings from tithing, but it does not take forever. It will take time for some of the messes in our lives to be straightened out, but it will not take forever. It will take time for us to get over some of our pain and hurt, but if you let Jesus into your life, it will not take forever.

So if you haven't gotten over your Nazareth yet, keep on growing. It won't take forever. If people are still reminding you of the mistakes you once made and what you used to be, keep on growing. It won't take forever for their comments not to matter. If people are still hurting your feelings and making you cry, keep on growing. They won't be hurting your feelings forever. You will reach a point where you will hear negative things and shake them off like dust from your feet, and you'll keep on growing and going forward while they stand still and talk. If you are still struggling with some issues, keep on growing. You will not be struggling with those issues forever. If you are still trying to get over some pain, keep on growing. The wounds will not be fresh forever. Keep growing until nothing in your past matters.

Take the Brakes off (for Growth)!

TEXT: MARK 6:1-6

I RECEIVED MY driver's license back in 1964, but the first car I owned was 1948 Mercury. Then I drove a 1950 Chevy for a while before moving on up to a 1957 Dodge Royal Lancer, all in one year. Since the Royal Lancer was the first car I owned that was less than ten years old when I procured it, I considered it practically new. It was about a city block long, two outhouses wide. It had these major tail fins, a V-8 engine, and a four-barrel carburetor. It used to pass everything on the road except a gas station. In addition, everything on it, including the gears, was push button. Every car has certain things that stand out about it. My Mercury stood out because it used to drink a quart of oil a day. The Chevy had no muffler, so you could hear me coming from two blocks away. And it did have a big dent in the door on the driver's side because a telephone pole was not polite enough to move out of the way when I was trying to get past it.

The Dodge Royal Lancer stands out because it was the car that really taught me about the care and maintenance a car should have. I drove it so much that toward the end of its life with me, it began to give me a little trouble. One day when I was in a hurry, I hopped into it, turned on the ignition, pushed the gear into drive, and pressed down on the gas. But instead of moving smoothly forward, it had a jerky motion, similar to what one feels when one is learning how to drive a stick shift. I pressed down on the gas again, and again the car jerked forward. I sat there for a moment trying to figure out what was wrong. I began to say to myself that I was going to have to get rid of this car as soon as I could when I looked down near my left knee and discovered that my emergency brake was on. There was nothing wrong with the car; the problem was with the driver. I was trying to drive with the emergency brake on. Once I took the brake off, the car moved smoothly ahead without any problem.

I fear that many of us are living with our brakes on. We are living with our faith brakes on. We are living with our self-confidence or self-esteem or insecurity brakes on. We are living with our giving brakes on. God has a great vision for your life and my life. God probably has a greater vision for us than we have for ourselves. However, to reach the vision God has for our lives, all of us will have to do some mental and spiritual growing. But since our growth brakes are on, God cannot take us to where God wants us to be. For God does not grow us against our will. Sometimes we look at the lives of others, the careers of others, the relationships of others, and we wish the same for ourselves. What we don't realize is that God has blessings for us that may go beyond what we see in the lives of others if only we would take the brakes off.

Are you saying, preacher, that God has a husband or wife for me just like someone else may have? Are you saying that God has the same happiness for me or the same material possessions or financial prosperity for me that someone else has? No, I am not. But what I am saying is that since nobody knows how happy another person really is—except that person and God—and since nobody but they and God know how much restful sleep at night anybody else is getting, and since nobody knows what goes on behind closed doors but the persons involved and God, then God might have a vision for your life and more real happiness and joy for your life than someone else seems to have. Whatever God has done in the lives of others that is good, positive, self-affirming, blessed, spiritual, righteous, uplifting, empowering, and healthy, God desires to do in each of our lives, but we have to take the brakes off. Whatever miracles God wrought in the Bible, whatever transformations in the lives of people God made in the Bible, whatever anointing or power or gifts God bestowed in the lives of some people in the Bible, God desires to do in our lives if we would just take the brakes off.

However, because many of us are still living with our brakes for growth on, I fear that a number of us will end up like the people of Nazareth in the text. Because they had their brakes of cynicism, close-mindedness, and narrow vision on, Jesus could do no mighty miracles in their midst and could foster no great growth in their lives. Although Nazareth was Jesus' hometown and the place where his family still resided, by the time he returned, we see in the text, he had already established his ministry.

He returns to Nazareth in chapter 6 of Mark's Gospel. In chapter 1 of this Gospel he had healed a man of an unclean spirit in Capernaum, had healed Peter's mother-in-law of a fever, and during the evening of that same day had cured a number of persons with various diseases. The first chapter ends with the account of his healing of a leper. In chapter 2 Jesus heals a paralytic and teaches. In chapter 3 he heals a man with a withered hand, teaches a multitude by the sea, and empowers twelve disciples to preach and to have authority over demons. In chapter 4 he teaches and stills a raging storm at sea. In chapter 5 he heals the Gerasene demoniac and a woman who simply touches the hem of his garment and is healed. And a dead girl is restored to life.

Thus by the time Jesus returns to his home in chapter 6, he had already established himself as an individual in whose life the power of God and the anointing of God was at work in special ways. When one considers all that Jesus had already done, one would think that his hometown people would have had their brakes of doubt and cynicism off and would have been ready to receive all that he offered. However, when he began to teach in their synagogues and do what he had done elsewhere, we are told that they were astounded. They said: "We had no idea he was this good. How did he get so wise all of a sudden, get such ability?" But in the next breath they were cutting him down. "He's just a carpenter: Mary's boy. We've known him since he was a lad. We know his brothers: James, Joses, Judas, and Simon. And his sisters. Who does he think he is?" They tripped over what little they knew about him and fell sprawling. And they never got any farther. Jesus told them, "A prophet has little honor in his hometown, among his relatives, on the streets he played in as a child." Jesus wasn't able to do much of anything there. He laid hands on a few sick people and healed them, that's all. He couldn't get over their stubbornness. He left, and then made a circuit of the other villages teaching.

At this point in our lives the track record of Jesus should be firmly established. We should be able to point to some definite things that have happened as a result of our faith in God and in prayer. We have prayed and things have changed; we have changed and miracles have been wrought. Some of us can look at ourselves and remember when the Lord made a definite change in us, in our personalities, in the way we live and think, in what we do with our time, and in what our priorities are. At this point the brakes in our lives for growth ought to be off, and we ought to be prepared to go wherever the Lord takes us. Yet so many of us have our brakes on still. We are trying to continue this Christian journey with our brakes on. The result is that our ride is jumpy and jerky, and we really are not going anywhere.

Some of us have our brakes of giving on. We just refuse to tithe. We have made up our minds that we are going to give only so much and that's all. And no matter what the preacher says, no matter how many tithing testimonies we hear, no matter what the Word of God says, no matter how many other people are doing it, we have put the brakes on. God gets only so much and that's it. And because we have put the brakes on our giving, our further growth is going to be jumpy and jerky, and we will grow only so much and get only so much from God. For as I have said before, God does not give the fullness of his blessings to those who rob him, who hold back from him, who put the brakes on with him. We want God to give us everything God has in store for us, yet we want to put the brakes on what we give. Because God is good, we will receive some blessings. Jesus healed a few sick people in Nazareth. We will get a few prayers answered. We will continue to receive God's blessings in our lives. But the mighty works, the great growth, and the great blessings God has in store for us will not come into our lives as long we have the brakes on in terms of our giving.

Some of us have the brakes on in terms of our faith. Perhaps that's why we don't tithe: because we don't see or understand how God will provide for us if we give ten percent of our gross income when we look at our bills and financial obligations. But it is not up to us to see or understand; it is up to us to believe. If we can see and understand, it's not faith, but sight. You don't need faith for what you can see; faith is about believing even when you don't see at that particular moment. It is not up to us to see or understand how God will bless; it is up to us to believe that God *will* bless. And when we look at the chapters in our lives that we have already lived and wherein the Lord has blessed, we ought to have enough faith to know that God will keep his Word and that God will supply all of our needs according to his riches in glory. God will do it not because the preacher says so, but because God's Word says so.

We ought to know by now that God will take care of us. God took care of us and watched over us before we became as close to him as we are now. God took care of us and watched over us before we became saved. God took care of us and watched over us when we were out in the world doing what we thought we were big enough and grown enough to do. God took care of us when we took foolish chances and when we made foolish mistakes. If God took care of us then, surely God will do the same for us now that we are trying to do what his Word instructs us to do. We need to take the brakes off of our faith and simply believe God based upon our experience with God's care, keeping, and way-making provision. We need to take the brakes off of our faith in God's Word because it is the Word of a God who always keeps his promises. The Bible says that Jesus could not get over the stubbornness of the people in Nazareth. Don't be stubborn. Quit resisting the Word of God. Quit resisting the Spirit of God that desires to bring you into new places.

We need to take the brakes of comfort off. I fear that many

of us are so far from where we started and have so much more than what we thought we would have that we are simply content to be where we are. We feel that if we keep striving and trying to grow and to get more, that we are being greedy or unthankful. We don't understand yet that God gets pleasure in giving to his children. It is God's desire to bestow the riches of the kingdom on his children. God does not get tired of his children asking, and God does not get tired of blessing his children. God wants his children to continue to grow, to continue to strive for the best, for excellence, and for all of the good things that life has to offer. When God sees so many of the people of the world doing well in this life, know that God also wants his children to do well in this life, to live healthy lives, to be financially prosperous, to have joy, and to have happiness. But God wants us to do well *his* way.

People of the world who do well and prosper in this life, their way, will not do well eternally. For when we do well our way, we don't give God the glory. That's why Herod was stricken as he sat upon the throne enjoying political success and the accolades of the crowd. The Bible says that he did not give God the glory. For it is appointed unto all persons once to die and after death the judgment. If you don't believe me, ask the rich farmer in Luke 12:15-21. He did so well that his barns were not big enough to hold all he had, and so he decided to tear them down and build bigger ones. Then he said to himself, "Soul, you have ample goods laid up for many years; relax, eat, drink, be merry." But God said to him, "You fool, this very night your life is being demanded of you. And the things you have prepared, whose will they be?" Jesus concludes, "So it is with those who store up treasures for themselves but are not rich toward God."

However, when we do well God's way, we not only have joy and blessings in this life, but happiness and blessings eternally. Paul said, "For to me to live is Christ, and to die is gain" (Philippians 1:21, KJV). Paul, paraphrasing Isaiah, wrote, "What no eye has seen, nor ear heard, nor the human heart conceived, what God has prepared for those who love him" (1 Corithians 2:9).

We need to take the brakes off of our comfort and know that

wherever we are, God has more for us. When we look at the power of God and God's desires for us, what God has done for us—no matter how miraculous it seems in our eyes—is equivalent to Jesus laying hands on a few sick people in Nazareth. It's wonderful. We thank God and give God the glory for what God has done. But God has some other mighty works, some other mighty miracles, and some other mighty blessings that God desires to bestow upon us if we would just take the brakes off of our comfort. If we could just take our eyes from the rearview mirror for a moment and start looking forward, we would learn that God not only has brought us a mighty long ways, but God still wants to take us a mighty long ways, if we would just take the brakes off.

Some of us have our brakes of fear on. For centuries people looked out over the ocean and dared to go only so far out because they believed that the world was flat and if they sailed out too far they would fall over the edge of the world into nothingness. But one day some Africans in some long boats decided to venture out farther than they could see. They went beyond the horizon and instead of falling off of the edge of the earth they discovered whole new worlds. So many of us are afraid to venture any farther than what we can see and go no further than what we already know. We are like the people in Nazareth who stumbled over what they knew about Jesus' background, family, and childhood and went no further. Don't let what little you know about Jesus—don't let what little experience you have with Jesus—stop you from going further with Jesus. I know you know him as a job provider, but he is so much more than that. I know you know him as a Savior, but he is so much more than that. I know you know him as a friend, but he is so much more than that. I know you know him as a healer, but he is so much more than that. I know you know him as Lord, but he is so much more than that. He is the very God, who created the ends of the universe, in human flesh. All of the lights of the stars of the universe pale before his glory. All of the darkness that is left in the universe after the stars go out cannot snuff out his light. All of the power that keeps every planet on its axis and propels every meteor in the universe cannot compare with his power. Death cannot hold him and the devil can't touch him. And the good news I bring is that a Savior with this much power and glory has a personal interest in you and in me, and he wants to grow us and take us to new places in him in this life and in eternity, places we cannot even begin to imagine. But we won't grow if we are afraid of change, if we are afraid of losing what little we have, if we are paralyzed by the "what ifs," and if we are afraid of the unknown. We may not know where the Lord is taking us, but we can trust Jesus. And if Jesus takes us there, we will be all right.

If Jesus wants us to give up something or sacrifice something, we will be all right. If Jesus causes us to lose something, we will be all right. We need to take off the brakes of fear and trust Jesus, who still does all things well. If we could just learn to trust Jesus, we would discover that when we sail with him as our captain, we do not fall over the edge of the world, but we sail into a whole new world.

The world will never know what things the people in Nazareth missed because they had their brakes of doubt and cynicism on. When we think about all Jesus did in other places, we can just imagine all he would have been glad to do there in Nazareth among his own people if they would have taken their brakes of shortsightedness off. When we think about how much the Lord has already done for us, we have no idea of how much he wants to do for us and will do for us if we would just let him, if we would just take the brakes of our giving, our faith, our comfort, and our fear off.

There are many definitions of hell. I have another one. Hell is standing beside Jesus with him showing us everything else he could have done for us, with our lives, and in our lives if we would have just let him, if we would have just taken off the brakes. Hell is seeing everything we missed out on because our brakes were on.

How does the passage that tells about the rejection of Jesus in his hometown of Nazareth end? Does it end with his statement about a prophet not being without honor in any land except his own? No! Does it end with his marveling at the unbelief of his hometown people? No! It ends with the statement that Jesus left Nazareth and went among other villages teaching. What Nazareth missed out on, other villages and other people in other places received. Our lack of vision, our unwillingness to grow, our negativity, our cynicism and doubt, our cheapness, our lack of faith has never stopped the Lord from blessing somebody else. I don't know about you, but I am selfish enough to want what the Lord has for me.

I don't want only others to get what the Lord also had for me but I didn't receive because I had my brakes on. I believe that you ought to be selfish in this regard also. I believe that you should want everything the Lord has for you: the growth, the power over demons, the peace, the blessings, the healing, and the wholeness. Are we prepared to take the brakes off today? Right here and right now? Take off your brakes. Receive all that the Lord has for you!